CONTENTS

KU-195-795

FOREWORD

BY PETE WINNER

I first became aware of the Special Air Service (SAS) Regiment when I was serving with 10 Airfield Construction Squadron Royal Engineers during the emergency in Aden in 1967 – my first operational tour of duty. There were all sorts of wild rumours flying around about what the regiment was up to, including undercover work, disguising themselves as locals, and ambushing the mad machine-gunners and grenade-throwing terrorists. It seemed far more exciting than being a spanner monkey and I was intrigued. Little did I know, as I went about my work repairing bulldozers that in less than five years I would be part of this elite organization and facing hundreds of communist shock troops re-supplied from this very area, namely, the port of Aden.

Then came the bad news that the British Army would be carrying out a tactical withdrawal from Aden, handing over all the camps, airfields and workshops to the communist regime. Towards the end of November 1967 the withdrawal began, and as 10 Squadron boarded the Hercules C-130 transport plane to fly us up to RAF Sharjah near Dubai, I could not shake off the feeling we were surrendering.

Over the next ten months I worked all round the area helping to build roads and helipads and it was during this period I had my first contact with 'The Regiment'. Every few weeks a group of SAS guys would appear in the cookhouse on camp and they were different from any soldiers I had seen before in the British Army. With their long hair, beards, different clothing and lack of badges of rank or insignia they looked like a gang of mercenaries. They also had an air of confidence about them, as if they owned the place. This was the first time I had seen SAS guys up close and they were impressive.

On camp the Royal Engineers had their own drinking club and it wasn't long before the SAS guys found out the club bar stayed open after the N.A.F.F.I. had closed. One late Saturday night a handful of the guys turned up at the club, took over the bar, and ordered drinks all round. The conversation flowed and I found out they were from 'Landrover troop', B squadron, and that's about all the information they parted with. They were more interested to find out if any of us wanted to come on selection and gave out details how to apply. It was only late into the night after we started to discuss what we regarded as the Aden fiasco that I became hooked on the idea of joining the Regiment.

The guys talked in general terms about the communist take over of the area, and hinted that 'something' was going to be done about it, but no place, names or timings were mentioned. It was all secret and very vague, but in the next couple of years, it all suddenly made sense. This was a chance to get my own back after that humiliating withdrawal. I made the decision there and then that I would put in for selection.

I immediately lodged my application form and spent the next couple of months training intensely. Success! I passed the initial three weeks' physical selection phase over the Brecon Beacons and then spent five more months on continuation training. This training included weapons and explosives training, first aid, resistance to interrogation training, and one month in the Far East on jungle training.

Out of the original 135 runners less than 15 of us presented ourselves at the Colonel's office to receive the famous beret and wings. I had cracked the greatest physical challenge of my life. I was now badged and, incredibly, I was posted to the very same 8 Troop, B Squadron.

I was pitched straight into squadron life and briefed on an operation that was going to take place in a few months to retake Dhofar, a province in southern Oman, from communist insurgents. My first SAS operation, and I was going to get a crack at the regime that humiliated the British Army back in 1967. Little did I know it would it would all end up with me fighting in the last conclusive battle against communism before the Berlin Wall came down.

The battle of Mirbat in July 1972 was a well-planned, determined attack by hundreds of communist shock troops against nine SAS soldiers – a modern-day Rorke's Drift that became famous within military circles but was a relatively unknown event in the eyes of the public.

Eight years later the SAS and myself would be pitched into an undeclared war on terrorism within the UK itself and within the full glare of the world's media. We had been training intensely for such an event so there was a general feeling of relief when the code that flashed on our personal alerters on the morning of 30 April 1980 was not a drill, it was for the real thing – a live operation. The Iranian Embassy in London had been taken over by terrorists claiming to be from the Front for the Liberation of Arabistan. B Squadron 22 SAS had just taken over the Special Projects (SP) Team from the previous squadron and we were raring to go. The Metropolitan Police took over the day-to-day running of the siege, declaring that a 'softly softly' approach would be maintained. However, when the terrorists' self-control finally disintegrated and the siege spiralled into violence we were called into action.

The following book reveals the careful planning that went into the SAS assault, the hours spent poring over building plans and the different assault options that were considered. It also gives a detailed blow-by-blow account from the abseiler's descent to the gathering of the freed hostages on the embassy lawn. Many books have been published detailing the events of 5 May 1980 but this volume corrects the multitude of errors that appear in most of these accounts, revealing the truth of exactly how we achieved what many consider the impossible.

For my part, I felt immense personal satisfaction and pride at being involved in such a successful military operation, undoubtedly one of the most significant actions of my entire military career. The day would live forever in regimental history. The victory had been gained, not only through faultless teamwork and infinite patience, but also through immense physical courage and flexibility in the face of overwhelming odds.

INTRODUCTION

Origins and functions of the SAS

In the course of less than a week in 1980, the Special Air Service (SAS), an elite special forces regiment of the British Army, emerged from almost total obscurity to become a household name in the United Kingdom and acquired instant recognition as the world's leading counter-terrorist unit.

Formed in 1941, in the midst of the World War II, the SAS came into being through the inspiration of Colonel David Stirling, a Scots Guardsman then convalescing in a hospital in Cairo from injuries sustained in a training accident. He envisioned an entirely new kind of unit, one divided into very small sub-units of four men each – of a sort not seen in any other regiment in the Army – where traditional notions of discipline and leadership did not apply. As he wrote years later:

> In the SAS each of the four men was trained to a high general level of proficiency in the whole range of SAS capability and, additionally, each man was trained to have at least one special expertise according to his aptitude. In carrying out an operation – often in pitch-dark – each SAS man in each module was exercising his own individual perception and judgement at full stretch. (Geraghty, *Who Dares Wins*, p. 8)

There was no 'leader' of this four-man team, in the traditional sense, whose members bonded like a family, the more so when two men were sometimes required to spend months together, day and night, often in isolation. They were to be completely classless, moulding their identity according to the warrior caste of the regiment and binding themselves together as a family. Stirling described the unit's philosophy thus:

> From the start, the SAS Regiment has had some firmly held tenets from which we never depart. They can be summarised as follows:
> 1. The unrelenting pursuit of excellence.
> 2. The maintaining of the highest standards of discipline in all aspects of the daily life of the SAS soldier (Geraghty, *Ibid.*, p. 9)

Stirling, a graduate of Cambridge, had joined a commando unit in 1940. Together with a fellow officer, Jock Lewes, an Oxford graduate from the Welsh Guards, he began to conceive of ways to strike at extended German supply lines in the Western Desert. When a misallocated supply of parachutes came into his possession, Stirling and Lewes, neither of whom were trained to use one, began experimenting. In an accident in which the canopy was shredded by the aircraft tailfin, Stirling descended at high speed to the ground, injuring his back so badly that both his legs were temporarily paralysed. While recovering in hospital, he laid out plans for the creation of a new unit that would penetrate deep behind enemy lines to perform strategic raids without the need for full-scale commando operations normally supported by air or naval units on a large scale. As the Long Range Desert Group was already performing this task in the desert by using vehicles, Stirling proposed a unit composed of saboteurs employing parachutes who could inflict damage on enemy airfields to an extent hitherto only carried out by large numbers of commandos.

With the approval of General Sir Claude Auchinleck, Commander-in-Chief, Middle East, the SAS was born. Many examples of derring-do followed in the Western Desert – though not without disastrous consequences in some cases – and the regiment was responsible for destroying hundreds of German aircraft on the ground and large quantities of military supplies and vehicles. Stirling himself was captured in Tunisia, and after several attempts to escape spent the rest of the war in Colditz. By this time the SAS consisted of two regiments, one in North Africa and the other operating in Sicily and along the Italian coast. By 1944 it was brigade-sized and had carried out numerous raids across the Mediterranean theatre. Thereafter it began to operate in occupied France, training and supplying the Resistance, harassing enemy communications by mining roads, blowing up railway lines, ambushing truck convoys and identifying targets suitable for air attack. Similar operations were later carried out in Holland, Denmark and in Germany itself. The two regiments were disbanded in October 1945 but were resurrected the following year.

The SAS remains the smallest corps of the British Army; whereas other elite units have come and gone according to wartime needs, the SAS remains as a permanent unit. It is unique in another way: it has evolved to take on a counter-revolutionary function, operating both at home and abroad, in small numbers and with disproportionate results, as it has demonstrated since 1945 in Malaya, Borneo, Oman, the Falklands, Northern Ireland, Iraq, Afghanistan and elsewhere.

The SAS did not have a counter-terrorist mandate until 1973 when the Counter Revolutionary Warfare (CRW) Wing was formed. Until that time the need for the development of counter-revolutionary training was recognized only as a result of a series of events that highlighted the need for the establishment of some sort of anti-terrorist squad; specifically, one more highly trained than the police and armed with specialist weapons and equipment. Indeed, prior to 1973 the exact role of the SAS in counter-revolutionary warfare had always been a matter of speculation and controversy for those outside the Army, not least because some of its operations had helped perpetuate the rule of undemocratic regimes in various parts of the world, principally in the Commonwealth. The *Land Operations Manual* (1969), a publication of the Ministry of Defence, spelled out its principal functions:

> SAS squadrons are particularly suited, trained and equipped for counter-revolutionary operations. Small parties may be infiltrated or dropped by parachute, including free fall, to avoid a long approach through enemy dominated areas, in order to carry out any of the following tasks:
> a. The collection of information on the location and movement of insurgent forces.
> b. The ambush and harrassment of insurgents.

    c.   The infiltration of sabotage, assassination and demolition parties into insurgent held areas.

    d.   Border surveillance.

    e.   Limited community relations.

    f.   Liaison with, and organization, training and control of friendly guerrilla forces operating against the common enemy.

Its low profile and the secret nature of its operations contributed further to perceptions that it was something other than a strictly military formation. In fact, the SAS did not and does not collect intelligence (except for purposes of fulfilling immediate military tasks while on campaign) and is not an arm of SIS (Secret Intelligence Service, or MI6), though informal links exist since intelligence officers occasionally require specialist military training which the SAS can provide. In short, the SAS is a regiment – albeit an extraordinary one – of the British Army, operating on a smaller scale than ordinary regiments, employing four-man patrols or 16-man troops, based at its headquarters near Hereford.

The purely operational role of the SAS began to change when, apart from those operating in Aden in 1967 and Dhofar (a region of south Yemen) in 1970–77, many SAS men were sent abroad to train the bodyguards of foreign heads of state whose death was thought to be adverse to British interests. In order to perform this new function, elements of the SAS began to train in a specially constructed house in which soldiers could practise shooting would-be kidnappers while avoiding hitting the VIP they were trained to protect. Formally known as the Close Quarter Battle (CQB) House, but informally as 'the Killing House', it was used to train bodyguards coming from overseas as well. These training schemes led to the creation of the Counter Revolutionary Warfare Wing, but when the SAS became fully committed in Dhofar, the regiment could no longer supply bodyguard training.

An expanded and somewhat ambiguous mandate of the CRW Wing, albeit limited by small numbers, came about as a direct result of the massacre that took place at the Munich Olympics in September 1972. With security relatively lax, a group of seven Palestinian terrorists known as 'Black September' was able to seize the dormitory occupied by Israeli athletes, killing two of them and taking nine hostage. The terrorists demanded the release of 200 Palestinians imprisoned in Israel. The Israelis flatly refused, but the West German government agreed to allow the gunmen, together with the hostages, safe passage out of the country. Matters unravelled at the airport, however, when German security forces opened fire and, in the fighting that ensued, all nine remaining hostages, five terrorists and one policeman were killed. Hundreds of millions of people watched the event on television, with dire political consequences for the West German government. Full media exposure not only embarrassed the West German authorities, but alerted other governments to the need to establish counter-terrorist units to cope with similar episodes that might arise in the future. In doing so, security organizations discovered that, paradoxically, the public tended to view the government and not the hostage-takers with disapprobation if the crisis ended in violence. This inspired Western governments, meeting at the G-7 summit talks the following year, to reach an agreement to establish forces specifically trained in counter-terrorism – not least because most countries had no military personnel trained to cope with a scenario like that at Munich.

The Germans were, quite naturally, keen to do so as quickly as possible, and established an anti-terrorist squad known at GSG-9. The French followed suit with their version, known as GIGN, the Americans created Delta Force and the British, recognising their own vulnerability to such a threat, decided that, while the

Metropolitan Police could be employed for such a task, its skills in this realm were necessarily limited, and therefore took the decision to establish a unit dedicated to counter-terrorism. In 1973, the Counter Revolutionary Warfare Wing of the SAS was expanded, with responsibility for serving not merely in its traditional role against insurgents abroad, but as the nation's hostage-rescue unit. This new task was perfectly logical, for in wartime the regiment had always performed this function. Specifically, in conducting such operations the SAS was trained to infiltrate an area by sea, land or air; gather intelligence about that area and the movement of hostile guerrilla forces; ambush and harass those guerrillas; assassinate and carry out demolition operations; conduct border surveillance; pursue a 'hearts and minds' policy; and train and liaise with friendly guerrilla forces. In their new function of hostage-rescue, hijack-busting and the relief of building sieges, they would no longer always wear military uniform, were trained in urban surveillance, close-quarter fighting and high-speed driving, and carried new forms of covert weaponry. Cross-service training also took place, so that when the CRW Wing was first deployed in January 1975 at Stansted Airport in response to an Iranian terrorist takeover of a civilian airliner, the team numbered about 20 men. The hijacker surrendered and was arrested without having inflicted any casualties. In December of the same year, the mere knowledge of the presence of the SAS on the scene was enough to induce two IRA terrorists to surrender themselves and release their two hostages at Balcombe Street, Marylebone, in central London.

The value of the CRW Wing was becoming clear, but its relationship with civilian institutions was not yet firmly established; specifically, the dual presence of police and soldiers on the scene at Balcombe Street first raised the question of who should have operational control. By the time of the embassy siege in 1980, this problem had been resolved through compromise: it was agreed that when a hostage situation was of an exclusively criminal nature, as at the Spaghetti House Restaurant in London in September 1975, the police would remain in complete operational control. Where a stand-off was of a political nature, however – that is, where the hostage-takers sought to coerce the British or any other government for political reasons – then the direction of negotiations and operations would fall to the responsibility of a Downing Street committee known as COBR (Cabinet Office Briefing Room; pronounced 'cobra'), assembled only in cases of emergency, such as a terrorist threat. The Home Secretary then and now chairs COBR, advised by senior Ministry of Defence, Cabinet Office and Foreign Office ministers, and representatives from the Metropolitan Police, MI5 (the security service responsible for domestic counter-intelligence), the SAS and other organizations and bodies. In this way, the SAS has direct access to senior government and police officials, together with operational connections to the police on the scene, who remain in tactical control while negotiations continue or until control is passed to the Ministry of Defence (MOD), with the SAS serving the function of Military Aid to the Civil Power (MACP), which the Army defines as:

> The provision of military assistance to the Civil Power [i.e. the government] in the maintenance of law, order and public safety using specialist capabilities or equipment, in situations beyond the capabilities of the Civil Power. Such assistance may be armed, if appropriate. For matters of public safety, support will routinely be given to the Police as the lead organization; this includes specific security operations.

Even during this period the SAS is stringently subject to the rule of law, with the rules of engagement carefully detailed in the tactical operations room established near the scene of the crisis. In this way the SAS plays no role in the negotiating phase of a siege, and thus is a politically neutral force whose sole function is to carry out military operations if these are deemed necessary. Nor is it in the interests of the SAS merely to go in 'with guns blazing', for their members are well aware that they could be prosecuted for using excessive force, and that the regiment's reputation could suffer as a result of the deaths of hostages, whether at the hands of the terrorists or, worse still, at those of the soldiers. In short, public perception that a military operation is heavy-handed could result in a disastrous political situation for the government and a propaganda victory for the terrorists. Much depends, therefore, on the training and equipment of the unit established to thwart hostage-takers.

Training and equipment

The SAS had years of training behind it, but no operational experience in handling a hostage-rescue situation. Opportunity arose, however, in October 1977 when two of its members, Major Alastair Morrison and Sergeant Barry Davies, led an assault team from GSG-9 in the rescue of German hostages held by Palestinian terrorists on a Lufthansa airliner in Mogadishu, Somalia. Further operational experience was gained by SAS advisers during the South Moluccan train siege in Holland in the same year. Finally, experience was gained during joint exercises with the American Delta Force and the French special forces unit, GIGN. At the time, the SAS CRW team was little more than 20-strong, but the Callaghan government, appreciating the success achieved in the Mogadishu raid, authorized a substantial increase to the CRW force and additional funds for improved equipment, including weapons and communications.

Thereafter, each SAS squadron trained in a CRW role on a rotating basis, between tours in Northern Ireland and training missions abroad. The permanent CRW wing would train all other SAS men, with the Special Projects (SP) Team carrying out siege-busting exercises, generally with a new scenario on each occasion, followed by a lengthy debriefing, known as a 'wash-up'. Once its training was complete, the same squadron would remain on standby and assist the next squadron's retraining in carrying out CRW exercises. This method of instruction proved its worth only two years later, when it was discovered at the Iranian Embassy siege that the entire squadron (approximately 80 men), consisting of two teams – Red and Blue, on 24-hour standby – was required for this substantial task, whereas the original team of 20 could not have coped with the situation. Thus, by 1980, the SAS had evolved to play a role that no other institution in Britain could fulfil, including the police. By the time of the embassy siege in 1980, the SP Team had had seven years in which to prepare for just such an eventuality; indeed, the sort of scenario for which they had tirelessly trained very closely matched that which they actually faced.

In the course of their training the SAS established a hostage scenario in which the basic features remain the same, apart from the type of location. First, the terrorists seize hostages and hold them in a building, an aircraft, a train, a bus or aboard a ship. Second, the police surround the location and begin to negotiate, offering small concessions – such as media coverage of the terrorists' demands – as a substitute for actually meeting those demands. Implicit in such a scenario is the notion that terrorism is, at its heart, psychological warfare in which public opinion can be shaped, and that security forces do not use what may popularly be perceived as excessive force lest a victory go to the terrorists. Moreover, the authorities must remain aware that the situation may be complicated by the fact that the terrorists' demands may not be directed at the British government, but rather at a foreign one, thus drastically limiting Whitehall's degree of influence over the situation. Next, with communications reaching deadlock, the terrorists threaten to kill a hostage; later, shots are fired by the terrorists inside their position, and the body of a hostage is

produced as evidence of their resolve to achieve their aims. The terrorists then issue a timetable of executions, which in turn finally triggers the SAS assault.

At SAS headquarters in Hereford all members of the regiment's Sabre (combat) Squadrons took part in a close-quarter battle (CQB) course, part of which involved training in the six-room 'Killing House', where hostage-rescue skills could be practised and refined. The main purpose of this training was to develop fine-tuned skills in entering a terrorist-held structure by a variety of means and, once inside, to distinguish instantly between terrorist and hostage, a situation made even more complex if a terrorist pretends to be a hostage. The 'Killing House', complete with furniture,

The Prime Minister standing outside the Killing House with members of the SP Team, having just watched a demonstration of room combat and hostage rescue.

contained standard NATO paper targets in the form of Russian soldiers representing terrorists, and others representing hostages, which were moved from place to place. The SP Team was divided into two specialist groups: the assault group, which stormed the building; and the perimeter containment group, which played the role of snipers who circled the scene and prevented anyone leaving (or entering), not only at ground level, but by way of the sewers or over the roofs. Assault groups usually operated in pairs, bursting into a room, instantly firing two pistol rounds (known as a 'double tap') or short, controlled bursts of automatic fire into each terrorist, aiming for the head, without injuring other SAS men or the hostages. Each two-man team was assigned a specific room to clear, with each man issued with explicit instructions about the direction in which he directed his fire so that, once a room was cleared and the next team came through, the likelihood of firing on colleagues was greatly reduced. If hit, a soldier was to wait for a medic to assist him when the operation was over.

The basic rule in assault is that laid out by Paddy Mayne, one of the founders of the SAS: 'When you enter a room full of armed men, shoot the first person who makes a move, hostile or otherwise. He has started to think and is therefore dangerous...' Some targets were of kneeling figures, sometimes arrayed behind furniture. Once perforated, patches and glue were applied over the bullet holes so the targets could be reused. Every man was regularly trained with live ammunition in order to hone his skills and reflexes in action so that if a terrorist uses a hostage as a shield, the SAS man can shoot the terrorist in the head without harm being done to the hostage. The SAS man must exhibit lightning reflexes and the ability to shoot accurately while running, crouching or rolling across the floor.

A member of the regiment described the kind of drills conducted at the time of the embassy siege:

Inside the 'Killing House' live ball ammunition is used all the time, though the walls have a special rubber coating which absorbs the impact of rounds as they hit. Before going into any hostage scene or other scenario, the team always goes through the potential risks they may face. The priority is always to eliminate the immediate threat. If you burst into a room and there are three terrorists – one with a knife, one holding a grenade and one pointing a machine gun – you always shoot the one with the gun, as he or she is the immediate threat.

The aim is to double tap the target until he drops. Only head shots count – in a room that can sometimes be filled with smoke there is no room for mistakes. Hits to the arms, legs and body will be discounted, and constant drills are required to ensure shooting standards are high. If the front man of the team has a problem with his primary weapon, which is usually a Heckler & Koch MP5 sub-machine gun, he will hold it to his left, drop down on one knee and draw his handgun. The man behind him will then stand over him until the problem with the defective weapon has been rectified. Then the point man will tap his mate's weapon or shout 'close', indicating that he is ready to continue with the assault. Two magazines are usually carried on the weapon, but magnetic clips are used as opposed to tape. Though most of the time only one mag is required, having two together is useful because the additional weight can stop the weapon pulling into the air when firing.

The aim is to slowly polish your skills as a team so that everyone is trained up to the same level, thinking on the same wave length and [being] aware of each other's actions. The 'House' is full of corridors, small rooms and obstacles, and often the scenario demands that the rescue be carried out in darkness (a basic SOP [standard operating procedure] on a live mission is for the power to be cut before the team goes into a building). The rooms are pretty barren, but they can be laid out to resemble the size and layout of a potential target, and the hostages will often be mixed in among the gunmen. Confidence in using live ammunition is developed by using 'live' hostages, who are drawn from the teams (the men wear body armour but no helmets). They usually sit at a table or stand on a marked spot, waiting to be 'rescued'. The CQB range also includes electronically operated figures that can be controlled by the training staff. At a basic level, for example, three figures will have their backs to you as you enter the room. Suddenly, all three will turn and one will be armed. In that split second you must make the right assessment and target the correct 'body' – if you don't you will 'kill' a hostage and the gunman will 'kill' you.

A variety of situations can be developed by the instructors. For example, they may tell the team leaders to stand down minutes before a rescue drill starts, forcing the team members to go through on their own. Other 'funnies' include smoke, gas, obstacles to separate team members from their colleagues, as well as loudspeakers to simulate crowd noises and shouting. (Crawford, *The SAS at Close Quarters*, pp. 66–68)

Apart from sub-machine guns and automatic pistols, shotguns, such as the Remington 870 pump-action model, were used to blow off door hinges and locks, though in exercises blanks were used for this purpose. An SAS soldier also had at his disposal a specially designed grenade, the G60 'flash-bang', consisting of mercury and magnesium powder, designed to blind and deafen an opponent for a few seconds – long enough to enable the SAS man to shoot him before he recovered from the effect. The weapon had first been used operationally at Mogadishu three years before. Each man also carried a personal radio with built-in microphones in the form of a headset so that the operation could be controlled and co-ordinated even amidst the smoke, darkness and noise. SAS men were also trained in abseiling – one aspect of their mountain training programme – which could be applied to hostage situations, and in the use of explosives, in order to blast their way into locked or fortified buildings. SAS teams also carried assault ladders consisting of differing widths to suit particular operational needs in a siege situation. These were black, custom-made in single or multi-sectional and extending types, fashioned from heavy-duty aluminium alloy with rungs deeply serrated, fitted with non-slip rubber feet and covered in noise-reducing buffers on all exposed sides. Such ladders allowed silent climbing for scaling walls as well as rapid access to buildings, vehicles, ships, aircraft, trains and buses.

The Special Projects Team was also equipped with specialized motor vehicles and aircraft, with which they could deploy themselves and their equipment anywhere in Britain. Other specialized equipment could be used to determine the location of hostages and gunmen inside a building: rooms could be scanned from the outside with a thermal imager, and fibre-optic equipment could be threaded into a room from an adjoining room, for instance, to view events without the occupants' knowledge. The SP Team could also potentially overhear conversations on various types of listening devices and thus, possibly, fix the positions of the hostage-takers. Whatever the scenario and equipment required, the SP Team was, and remains to this day, on continuous and immediate standby – with each trooper carrying a bleeper and a holdall packed with assault gear.

WEAPONS AND EQUIPMENT

1 Assault suit

2 Body armour

3 Assault belt rig

4 Regimental cap badge

5 Respirator

6 Stun grenade ('flash bang')

7 Browning 9mm high-power pistol, clip and ammunition

8 Heckler & Koch MP5 sub-machine gun, clips and ammunition

   Weight: 2.55 kg (4.4 lb)

   Calibre: 9mm x 19 Parabellum

   Muzzle velocity: 400m (436 yards) per second

   Magazine capacity: 15- or 30- round, box

   Rate of fire: 650 rpm

9 Remington 870 pump action shotgun

ORIGINS OF THE RAID

Motives for the attack

On the morning of 30 April 1980 six Iraqi-backed Iranian revolutionaries assembled in the foyer of their hotel at 105 Lexham Gardens in Kensington, in London's West End, and left the building en route to the Iranian Embassy in Princes Gate, South Kensington. They belonged to a group calling itself the Democratic Revolutionary Front for the Liberation of Arabistan, which sought independence for an oil-rich region in south-western Iran known officially as Khuzestan, whose inhabitants are ethnic Arabs, not Persians, with a history of revolt against Iran. By dint of its oil, Khuzestan is the source of Iran's wealth, having been developed by British and American companies before and during the Shah's reign, which ended with the Islamic revolution in early 1979. At that time the country was exporting five million barrels of Khuzestani oil a day – about one-tenth of the world's oil production. Without Khuzestan, Iran is incapable of being more than a minor power. Most of its Arab inhabitants call it 'Arabistan', a region that came into Persian hands by a territorial swap in 1847 by which the Ottoman Empire ceded it to Persia in exchange for part of Kurdistan (now Iraqi Kurdistan), since the Kurds were Sunni Muslims, like most Ottoman subjects, while Khuzestanis were Shi'a Muslims, like most Persians.

Notwithstanding their shared faith, Khuzestanis were not reconciled to Persian overlordship, and maintained until 1925 a degree of local autonomy under their own Arab sheiks. Thereafter, the Shah's father, Reza Shah, began a campaign of suppression to stamp out their autonomy and resettle Persian speakers in the region. The Khuzestanis rebelled after World War II in a bid to link themselves with Iraq, but were put down, remaining in this state until 1978, when oil workers in Khuzestan went on strike and cut the flow of oil to Tehran, contributing decisively to the downfall of the Shah and the onset of the Islamic Revolution. Any hopes of self-rule were dashed by the new regime, however, for the Ayatollah had no desire to see the new Islamic state partitioned into ethnically homogeneous regions – with Persians still a dominant majority, but separated from the Kurds in the west, Turkish-speaking Azerbaijanis in the north-west, Baluchis in the south-east and Khuzestanis in the south-west. In frustration, the Khuzestanis began a campaign of violence and destruction, inflicting widespread damage to the oil industry of Iran and reducing exports considerably below a million barrels a day – an 80 per cent decline. Herein lay the motive behind those who seized the Iranian Embassy in London: an opportunity – with the full attention of the world's media and London's large Arab community – to publicize their cause, grab headlines and trumpet their grievances which were largely unknown to the Western public.

This was not to be achieved simply by holding hostage the diplomatic staff of the Iranian Embassy; it was a deliberate measure to give Tehran a taste of its own medicine, for it was the logical parallel to the Iranian takeover of the US Embassy in Tehran that had occurred the previous year. The seizure of the embassy in London led to Iran's immediate condemnation of the act as a conspiracy involving Iraq, the CIA and MI6. Such a sweeping and unsubstantiated claim succeeded in further alienating the Islamic Republic in the eyes of the West, and thus played into the hands of the Khuzestani separatist cause. It did not succeed, nor did it lead to the release of the American hostages, which in any event was never its purpose, but it did widely publicize the terrorists' cause, one of their principal objectives.

**APRIL 30
1980**

**1125hrs:
Six armed terrorists
seize the Iranian
Embassy**

Yet the embassy siege cannot be fully appreciated without considering the broader context of Arab-Iranian relations, for the Arab world viewed the new regime in Tehran with suspicion and fear, regarding the Ayatollah as not merely a fervent defender of the Islamic faith, but a visionary on the edge – a mad reactionary seeking to return Iranian society and culture to the form it had originally taken in the 8th century, during the introduction of Islam to the Middle East, while simultaneously condemning Western values as satanic.

To his Arab neighbours, the Ayatollah represented a dangerous form of fanaticism and anarchy – a direct threat to their rule, especially the secular dictatorships like Iraq – not least because of his belief that clerics, including himself, should rule by divine right, a principle that rendered secular regimes hypocritical and illegitimate. No sooner had the revolution in Iran succeeded than clerics began a campaign of renewing Persian-Arab hostility, a feature of the region extending back more than a millennium, with the rift exacerbated by the fact that Iranians are largely Shi'as, whereas the ruling minority in Iraq were exclusively Sunnis. Iran's revolution, like all radical political movements, was not intended simply to apply to a domestic context, but was to be exported, giving rise to grave concerns not merely in Iraq, but in Saudi Arabia, the Gulf States and elsewhere in the region. Nor were such anxieties without some foundation: from the outset, Iran openly condemned as false Muslims a number of neighbouring governments, saving the greatest vitriol for Iraq, which increasingly turned to whatever measures, including violence, it believed would curb Iranian missionary zeal.

Relations between the two states had never been close, not least because Iraq's predominantly Shi'a population was ruled – and traditional suppressed by – a Sunni

Burning of the American flag on top of the US Embassy in Tehran, 4 November 1979. The Iranian Government erroneously believed that the attack on their own embassy in London six months later constituted a US-backed retaliatory operation using Khuzestani separatists to do their dirty work. (Corbis)

minority under the ruthless Saddam Hussein, who was well aware that many Iraqi Shi'as looked to Iran for support. Nor is Iraq the exception: in Saudi Arabia, where Sunnis run the country, the rich oil-bearing region in the east of the country is Shi'a, and might conceivably have turned their allegiance to Khomeini. Bahrain, a tiny island-state in the Persian Gulf, is predominantly Shi'a, yet ruled by Sunni sheiks. Complicating matters still further, southern Iraq is the site of the holiest Shi'a cities – Najaf and Karbela – as significant to their respective populations as Jerusalem is to Jews and Rome is to Catholics. Indeed, for 15 years of his exile the Ayatollah lived in Najaf. To Iraq, therefore, if ancient religious ties bound Shi'as together more powerfully than did nationality – with the modern nation-states of the Middle East dating their existences no further back than the fall of the Ottoman Empire after World War I – Saddam could face a revolution himself, possibly backed by an Iranian regime which openly offered aid to fellow Shi'as. Having effectively governed Iraq since 1968, Saddam was not about to concede the reins of power to Shi'a nationalism, a revived Persian state and a volatile theocracy openly condemning secular modernism. Pride almost certainly played its part in this growing political and ideological rivalry, for Saddam regarded himself as the new Nasser of the Middle East, backed by $30 billion in annual oil revenue, an army of a

The Ayatollah Khomeini, political and religious leader of Iran, returned to his country from exile in February 1979. His government correctly deduced that Iraq lay behind the takeover of the Iranian Embassy in London, an act which contributed to the rapidly deteriorating relations between the two countries which would result in a bitter and appallingly costly eight-year conflict (1980–88). (Getty)

quarter of a million men (as opposed to the grossly inefficient Iranian Army, whose officers had largely fled or been executed, not unlike the situation facing Royalist officers in France in the 1790s) and a leader with a Stalinist grip over his people. Such a leader was unlikely to permit a new challenger for regional hegemony, especially when Saudi Arabia, Kuwait and the other wealthy yet vulnerable Gulf States increasingly viewed Saddam – albeit with a degree of suspicion – as a bastion against Islamic extremism.

The denunciation of each other's regimes was only the start of the growing rift between Tehran and Baghdad in 1979; soon, both sides began to call for the other's overthrow, and trained and supported agents pursuing a policy of sabotage and assassination across the border, with the Iranians backing an 'Islamic Liberation Army' consisting of Shi'as from southern Iraq, and Saddam supporting calls for Khuzestani autonomy by sending armed men into the region to finance, train and equip its dissidents, and to blow up police stations, bridges and oil installations – all in a bid to erode the Ayatollah's authority. Territorial jealousies did not end there, for Saddam also wished to recover control of the Shatt al-Arab, the vital 120-mile (192km) waterway formed by the confluence of the Tigris, Euphrates and the Iranian river Karum, which empties at the head of the Gulf at the Iraqi port of Basra.

The attack on the Iranian Embassy must therefore be seen in the context of the growing political tensions between Iran and Iraq between 1979 and 1980 that would later reach their climax in a bitter eight-year conflict, which began several months after the crisis at Princes Gate. In the meantime, the seizure of the embassy offered a high-profile method of striking at Iran in a city with lax security, a large, hopefully sympathetic Arab community, and an international press corps eager to televise events for the court of world public opinion.

THE SEIZURE OF THE EMBASSY

Day One: Wednesday, 30 April 1980

The six revolutionaries making their way to Princes Gate had arrived in London from Iraq a month before, together with their handler, who had flown back the same day having overseen their training in Baghdad. In the course of their stay they had spent considerable sums on electronics and other goods to be shipped to Iraq – doubtless a form of payment for their efforts. The men were well armed but poorly trained in the use of their Soviet RGD-5 grenades, automatic pistols and Polish machine guns – almost certainly infiltrated into the United Kingdom in the Iraqi diplomatic bag – possibly because whoever sent them did not expect them to require their use. Even if success could not be achieved, the mission would provide publicity for their political aim, which was to be explained to several Arab diplomats, before the safe return of the gunmen to Iraq.

In their holdalls the terrorists carried two 9mm SMG machine pistols; three Browning automatics with 13-round magazines loaded with Winchester hollow-point ammunition, a Polish-made Skorpion sub-machine gun, a .38 revolver and several Russian hand grenades. Thus heavily armed, the six men, with cloth pulled tightly around their heads, ascended the steps of the Iranian Embassy at 16 Princes Gate at 1125hrs, and burst into the building with weapons drawn. Their leader, known as Oan (Oan Ali Mohammed, also known by the police codename 'Salim') and the only member of the group who could speak English with reasonable fluency, immediately approached PC Trevor Lock, from the Diplomatic Protection Group, who was standing by the door to reception at the bottom of the stairs. Shouting, 'Don't move! Don't move!' in Farsi, Oan fired a deafening burst of sub-machine gun fire and tore Lock's radio from his tunic, though not before Lock had succeeded in transmitting an emergency signal to Scotland Yard with the aid of the 'panic' button on his radio. Confusion and disorder reigned. The embassy was now in the terrorists' hands, including 26 hostages: 17 members of embassy staff, eight visitors and Trevor Lock. Apart from Lock, the other British hostages were Sim Harris and Chris Cramer, employees of the BBC there to collect visas for a visit to Iran, and Ron Morris, the embassy manager and chauffeur. 'We are members of the Democratic Revolutionary Front for the Liberation of Arabistan. We are the Martyrs', Oan declared, referring to their alternative name, 'the Group of the Martyr'. He then issued the following demands: 'our human and legitimate rights'; autonomy for 'Arabistan'; the release of 91 Arabs being held in Iranian jails and safe passage for them out of Iran to the destination of their choice – presumably Iraq. If these demands were not met by noon on Thursday, 1 May, the embassy and all its occupants would be blown up.

The Metropolitan Police responded immediately and John Dellow, Deputy Assistant Commissioner, took immediate charge of the scene, establishing a temporary command post in his car and ordering his men to cordon off the area. He also called for the deployment of police terrorist dogs, housed at Heathrow Airport, which could be used if the terrorists attempted a mass breakout. Some consideration was given to the idea of establishing the police forward control room a few doors to the west of the embassy at no. 25, the offices of the Royal School of Needlework. Brigadier Peter de la Billière, Head of SAS Group, based in London, explained in his memoirs that:

… the ladies in charge there gallantly gave up their ground floor to an invasion of detectives and constables. But the place was cluttered with priceless artefacts – ancient tapestries, regimental colours in for repair, peers' coronation robes; worse, there was an absolute ban on smoking in the building. Dellow did not think his men could endure such a deprivation for days on end, and was forced to look for somewhere else.

He therefore established Alpha Control – the main police incident headquarters – down the terrace at no. 24, a Montessori nursery school which was quickly evacuated and the furniture removed. 'The only conditions laid on the police', de la Billière recalled, 'were that they should take care with the miniature lavatories in the basement, feed the hamster which was left in residence, and not molest a duck which was nesting on a windowsill.' Communications equipment and generators quickly arrived, and Dellow established his control room under the eaves in the attic. From here the police began to establish communication with the hostage-takers while simultaneously deploying specialist units to seal off the immediate area, including D11 police marksmen, known as the 'Blue Berets', who took up positions around the embassy, C13 anti-terrorist officers, the Special Patrol Group and members of C7, Scotland Yard's Technical Support Branch, which could deploy surveillance equipment with which to monitor sound and movement inside buildings. Contingency had also to be made for the possibility that the services of the SAS would be required, as circumstances might require resources beyond the capabilities of the police alone.

Using a green field telephone passed through a window on the ground floor of the embassy, the police soon established contact with Oan through their team of negotiators. The services of a Farsi interpreter – a woman who, quick at translation, was well regarded by the police – were rapidly secured, as well as a psychiatrist, whose training in criminology enabled him to brief the authorities on the terrorists' mood and likely course of action.

The large police presence naturally attracted public and press interest, and reporters flocked to the area, obliging the police not merely to evacuate the houses, flats, businesses and other embassies around the area, but to manage the situation by corralling the rapidly growing army of journalists and television teams into a small area about a hundred yards west of the embassy into what became known as 'Pressville'. This not only served to keep them safe from harm, but allowed the police unrestricted access to the area. It was also essential that reporters be kept at a distance, as it was imperative that the terrorists should not watch the police making their preparations on television. In the event, technical problems prevented the police from jamming television reception into the embassy, so Dellow instead considered erecting high screens against the houses near the embassy in an effort to block the television crews' view. The screens were duly made but never erected, as this might suggest to the terrorists that an assault was imminent. These measures would have been futile in any event, since the media camp brought in hydraulic bucket-hoists (known in the industry as 'cherry-pickers') to elevate their cameramen above

Peter de la Billière originally passed selection for the SAS in 1956, serving in Malaya and Oman, where he was Mentioned in Dispatches and awarded the Military Cross. Later he was appointed as the OC of A Squadron 22 SAS in Aden 1964–66, and was awarded a bar to his Military Cross. By the time of the Iranian Embassy Siege he was Director of Special Forces. In 1990 he was Commander-in-Chief British Forces in the 1990 Gulf War where he was influential in convincing General Norman Schwarzkopf to use special forces. He eventually retired in 1992. (Getty)

THE HOSTAGES

Dr Gholam-Ali Afrouz – *Chargé d'affaires, Iranian Embassy*

Shirazed Bouroumand – *Embassy secretary*

Chris Cramer – *BBC sound organizer*

Ahmed Dadgar – *Medical clerk*

Dr Abdul Fazi Ezzati – *Iranian Cultural Attaché*

Abbas Fallahi – *Embassy doorman*

Muhammad Hashir Faruqi – *British Pakistani; editor of the Muslim political magazine* Impact International

Ali Guil Ghanzafar – *Pakistani tourist*

Simeon Harris – *BBC sound recordist*

Mrs Nooshin Hashemenian – *Embassy secretary*

Miss Roya Kaghachi – *Secretary to Dr Afrouz*

Mrs Hiyech Sanei Kanji – *Embassy secretary; three months pregnant*

Mustapha Karkouti – *Syrian journalist working for Lebanese newspaper* Assafir

Vahid Khabaz – *Iranian student; part-time London correspondent of Tehran-based newspaper* Keyhan

Abbas Lavasani – *Chief Press Officer, Iranian Embassy*

Police Constable Trevor Lock – *Diplomatic Protection Group, Metropolitan Police*

Moutaba Mehrnavard – *Carpet dealer*

Aboutaleb Jishverdi-Moghaddam – *Iranian attaché*

Muhammad Moheb – *Embassy accountant*

Ronald Morris – *Embassy manager and chauffeur*

Mrs Frieda Mozafarian – *Press officer*

Issa Naghizadeh – *First Secretary*

Ali Akbar Samadzadeh – *Temporary employee of Embassy; graduate student in computer science*

Ali Aghar Tabatabal – *Banker*

Kaujouri Muhammad Taghi – *Accountant*

Zahra Zomorrodian – *Embassy clerk*

obstructions. Still, their view was restricted to the front of the embassy, for no easily accessible public vantage point existed to the rear.

The police were not solely involved. The Army, specifically the SAS, became aware of the crisis from the outset. Indeed, by coincidence, the SAS learned of the incident even before official notification was received, for at 1144 hours, an ex-D Squadron SAS corporal named Dusty Gray, then serving in the Metropolitan Police as a dog-handler, rang the 'Kremlin' (the nickname for SAS headquarters at Hereford) to provide Lieutenant-Colonel Mike Rose, Commanding Officer of 22 SAS, with the little information that he then had. Rose was at first sceptical, suspecting that the Home Office was trying to confuse him as part of a coming exercise in Northumbria. Gray insisted that this was no false alarm, that the police were on their way to Princes Gate and that the SAS would be required. Rose immediately contacted de la Billière in London, seeking confirmation from him, via the Ministry of Defence, that a major terrorist incident was in fact under way. In the event, Rose did not wait for confirmation, but ordered the Special Projects Team at Hereford, on 24-hour standby for anti-terrorist and hostage-rescue operations, to make itself ready to move.

At that moment, the team happened to be in the 'Killing House', shooting at the figure-eleven targets inside and about to deploy on an aircraft hijack exercise in the north-east drawn up by the Home Office and Northumbrian police. Operating in three teams of four, they were practising head shots, firing single shots or double taps only, with each man allocated a specific room to clear, and distracted by a flash of ISFE (instantaneous safety-fuse electric). Just as they were finishing, at 1148hrs, each

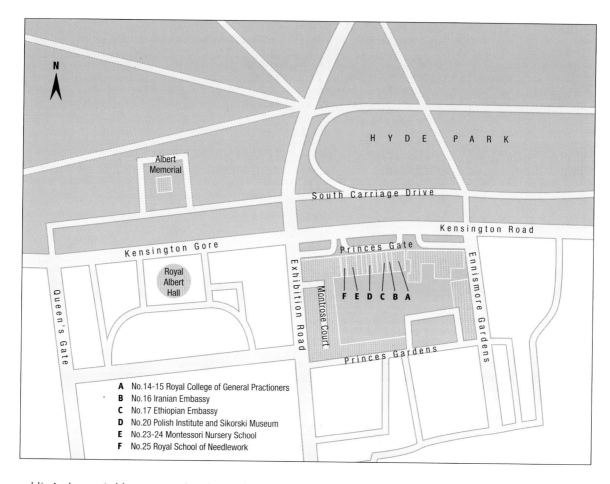

A No.14-15 Royal College of General Practioners
B No.16 Iranian Embassy
C No.17 Ethiopian Embassy
D No.20 Polish Institute and Sikorski Museum
E No.23-24 Montessori Nursery School
F No.25 Royal School of Needlework

soldier's electronic bleeper – an alert device that every member was required to carry and whose movements were restricted – sounded. Some thought it an error, not least because of the impending exercise, until notified otherwise: 'From Crocker. This is the real thing. Pack your gear, then move into the hangar for a brief.'

As de la Billière explained in his memoirs, 'When Whitehall failed to produce any definite reaction, Rose did not wait, but despatched his team immediately: away they went, outstripping bureaucratic obstruction and evading the Press, to pitch up for the time being at a hideaway in Beaconsfield, within easy reach of the capital.' Rose went ahead by helicopter to RAF Northolt, to the west of London, and drove into the capital in the Station Commander's car. He reached the scene in civilian clothes, introduced himself to Dellow and made a preliminary reconnaissance. Thus, six hours before the Ministry of Defence issued formal orders for the Special Projects Team, dressed in plain clothes, to proceed to west London, they had already left, travelling by white Range Rovers, and arriving in the early hours of 1 May at the holding area at their Regent's Park barracks.

While the police rapidly secured the area around Princes Gate, in Whitehall the Home Secretary, Willie Whitelaw, to whom the Prime Minister, then on a visit to the BBC, delegated authority, assembled a crisis management team in the Cabinet Office Briefing Room, which consisted of senior members of the Ministry of Defence, the Foreign Office, the Metropolitan Police, the Home Office, MI5, MI6 (the security and intelligence services), the public utilities, including the gas board, water board and British Airports Authority, as well as a representative of the SAS in the form of de la

APRIL 30
1980

1144hrs:
SAS informed
of situation

Billière, who arrived a few hours after reaching Princes Gate. De la Billière took a seat next to the Director of Military Operations, Major-General Derek Boorman, in COBR, a windowless and undistinguished room save for a battery of televisions and a small digital clock.

Thatcher explained the function of COBR in her memoirs: 'Hour by hour information is gathered, sifted and analysed so that every circumstance and option can be properly evaluated. Throughout the crisis, Whitelaw kept in regular contact with me.' The Prime Minister and Home Secretary also agreed on strategy. The police should initially begin with patient negotiation, but if any hostages were wounded, a military assault would be considered. However, if a hostage was killed, the SAS would definitely be sent in. Both Thatcher and Whitelaw recognized that there would need to be a degree of flexibility, but ruled out from the start that the hostage-takers be allowed to leave the country as free agents.

As this was not a straightforward criminal act, there were special circumstances at play, as Whitelaw explained in his memoirs:

> The international dimension of the problem presented a diplomatic, as well as a terrorist, challenge. Relations with Iran were difficult following the overthrow of the Shah in 1979. The new Islamic regime had still not fully stabilized. Forty-nine American hostages were being held hostage in Tehran and earlier that same month President Carter had ordered an abortive helicopter-borne raid in an attempt to free them. The Cabinet had recently been considering American requests that we should impose economic sanctions on Iran in view of their refusal to release the US hostages; emergency powers to this end were taken by legislation in May. It was thus not surprising that the diplomatic response from Iran was frosty. The Foreign Minister made it clear that Iran, for its part, would meet none of the terrorists' demands. Iran declared that if any hostages died an equal number of Iranian Arabs would be 'tried and executed'. The Foreign Minister also warned on 1 May that Britain would be 'held responsible for everything that happens to our diplomats.'

Although, the Prime Minister was not present, she nevertheless established three principles from the outset: first; the laws of the United Kingdom would be applied to the situation, notwithstanding the fact that the incident was taking place in a foreign embassy; second, the terrorists were under no circumstances to be allowed to leave the country; and third, a peaceful resolution was paramount, to which end the police were to negotiate for as long as necessary to achieve this. Thatcher was also clear about how to proceed, as she later recorded:

> The Iranian Government had no intention of conceding these [the terrorists'] demands; and we, for our part, had no intention of allowing terrorists to succeed in their hostage taking. I was conscious that, though the group involved was a different one, this was no less an attempt to exploit perceived western weakness than was the hostage taking of the American embassy personnel in Tehran. My policy would be to do everything possible to resolve the crisis peacefully, without unnecessarily risking the lives of the hostages, but above all to ensure that terrorism should be – and be seen to be – defeated.

Day Two: Thursday, 1 May

While COBR continued to meet and the police maintained their vigil around the embassy, in the early hours of 1 May both Blue Team and Red Team arrived at the Regent's Park Barracks in white Range Rovers, unpacked their assault kit, laid out

Faisal, Salim's second-in-command, collecting a message from a shoebox which has been attached to a long pole, held by a plain clothes policeman at the extreme left.

their weapons, opened boxes of ammunition and loaded their magazines. Staff Sergeant Pete Winner, later known as 'Soldier I' described the holding area as '... large, derelict and drafty. The toilets were blocked and there was only cold running water. Grey powdery dust clung to the floors, window ledges, and wash-basins, turning the whole building into a health hazard. I was lying on an army camp-bed, going over in my mind the details of the early-morning green-slime [Military Intelligence] brief we had just received.' From here they would move to the Forward Holding Area chosen by Mike Rose, the Royal College of General Practitioners at no. 14, next door to the embassy. Over the course of the afternoon Rose had discovered a concealed route into the building, through some flats at the back of Princes Gate, across a garden and along the communal basement passage which ran the length of the terrace, allowing the SAS to enter undetected.

At 0330hrs the 24 men of Red Team stealthily made their way into no. 14 unobserved, by which time Rose had already drawn up an 'immediate action plan' – made ready one hour after arriving at an incident and to be implemented if an assault were required at ten minutes' notice – for example, if the terrorists began killing hostages. Initially this could be no more sophisticated than smashing their way through the windows of the top floor and fighting their way downwards with sub-machine guns and CS gas, with the purpose of rescuing as many hostages as possible before a general massacre ensued. The method was crude, but was the only option available until a more considered approach to the problem could be worked out based on digested intelligence, especially the location of the terrorists within the embassy. However, when it appeared that no rescue attempt was imminent, a 'deliberate assault plan' was drafted in its stead, while Red Team had to remain on alert.

If the SAS *was* required to storm the embassy, the key to success lay in gathering accurate intelligence and rehearsing the attack based on that intelligence. Intelligence officers therefore examined every piece of information that could be gathered

MAY 1
1980

1115hrs:
Terrorists release
Chris Cramer

concerning the embassy, and consulted people who had recently visited the building, to learn of any recent alterations to the place and the positioning of large obstacles, such as furniture. By happy circumstance, years before, the SAS had been asked by the Shah's government to survey the whole building, assess its security and make recommendations for its improvement. The plans were pored over, but no one knew which, if any, of the recommendations had been adopted and what other changes to the building may have been made since the inspection. Specifically, the SAS had suggested that the Iranians fit armoured glass to the ground and first-floor windows; but whether such work had been carried out was unknown.

Nevertheless, on the basis of this wealth of information, police carpenters built a scale model of the first and second floors of the embassy – and later the entire building – hastily fabricated from quarter-inch plywood, with every room and corridor reproduced, with doors opening in the correct direction. Then, in a hangar at Regent's Park Barracks, the Pioneer Company of the Irish Guards began constructing a life-sized replica of each floor of the embassy from wood and hessian.

While this work was in progress Oan, though growing increasingly irritable, released one of the sick hostages, a woman named Frieda Mozafarian. He would not, however, release Chris Cramer, the BBC sound organizer, who had become violently ill, so the police refused to reciprocate by allowing a doctor access to the embassy to examine him. Oddly, the authorities had yet to cut international telephone communication, and thus Oan was able to call the Iranian Foreign Ministry in Tehran to learn from the Foreign Minister, Sadegh Ghotzbadeh, that the terrorists were regarded as agents of the Carter administration and the CIA, and that the hostages would doubtless be willing to sacrifice their lives as martyrs for the Islamic Revolution.

By late morning Oan faced the problem posed by an increasingly ailing Cramer, who was doubled up with severe stomach pains and suffering from a fever. Cramer called on Oan for a doctor, only to be told that the authorities had refused to supply one. Sim Harris, Cramer's BBC colleague, requested to speak to the police to try to overturn that decision. He was led downstairs to the green field telephone that the police had passed into the embassy in a shoebox secured to a long pole. The police negotiator promised to consider the request, but told Harris to persuade Oan to release Cramer instead. Harris continued to plead with the police for a doctor, and Cramer, growing increasingly ill, was assisted downstairs and laid on the floor of the embassy foyer, where he writhed in pain. Oan began to appreciate that Cramer was more of a liability than an asset and released him through the front door of the embassy at 1115hrs, when Cramer stumbled down the steps into a waiting ambulance. This was a tactical error on the part of the terrorists, for the police immediately debriefed the former hostage, enquiring into the number of gunmen, their weapons, the layout of the embassy and the location of the hostages.

Knowledge of the building's interior was growing apace and the police now sought real-time intelligence; permission was therefore sought for special access into no. 17, the Ethiopian Embassy next door, where men from MI5 began using hand drills to install microphones into the walls and to lower listening devices down the chimneys from the roof, for the purpose of identifying the positions of the terrorists and the hostages. When Oan asked Lock to identify this sound, which he regarded with suspicion, Lock, knowing full well what it represented, blamed mice in the cavities of the walls. Notwithstanding all these preparations, the entire operation was a daunting one, for the embassy consisted of five storeys above ground, plus a cellar, the whole structure containing more than 50 rooms. The solid Victorian construction also meant shared terraced walls of granite measuring 22 inches (55.9cm) on one side and 19 (48.3cm) on the other. The police needed a distraction to cover the sound of their work in the form of ambient noise. Within minutes, COBR made a request to the gas board representative sitting on the committee for road drilling to be carried out on a fictitious gas main near the embassy. This indeed produced a great deal of noise – explained to the terrorists as emergency repairs in response to the report of a gas leak in the street – but as it tended to unnerve the terrorists, the ruse was cancelled. Rose then tried an alternative: rerouting incoming aircraft bound for Heathrow to descend low over the southern boundary of Hyde Park. Very quickly this request bore fruit, with large numbers of aircraft flying at hitherto inconceivably low altitudes over a built-up area. At the same time, using as much stealth as possible, engineers removed bricks separating the Iranian and Ethiopian embassies one by one, leaving only a veneer of plaster for an assault team to burst through if circumstances required.

While Oan allowed the first deadline, as well as a second one of 1400 hours, to pass without incident, he nevertheless began to change his demands. He now wanted three ambassadors from Arab countries to serve as mediators and negotiate for a plane to take him and his men out of Britain. The notion of a foreign intermediary, however, did not sit well with the British government, as Thatcher explained in her memoirs: '... we were extremely doubtful about this: there was a risk that the objectives of such an intermediary would be different from our own. Moreover, the Jordanians, whom we *were* prepared to trust, refused to become involved.'

Day Three: Friday, 2 May

At 0330hrs, 24 hours after Red Team had assembled in no. 14 on continuous standby, Blue Team arrived to relieve them. Red Team retired unseen in vans to Regent's Park Barracks, where they took much-needed sleep before practising inside the makeshift rooms of the model embassy. Despite the presence of a large body of journalists in Kensington, the press was still unaware that the SAS was on the scene. By 0930hrs Oan was complaining that the police had cut off his access to telephone and telex communication in an attempt to deprive the outside of information about the terrorists' cause. In retaliation, Oan threatened to kill a hostage, and at gunpoint ordered Mustapha Karkouti, an Arab journalist, to bring him Dr Ezzatti, the Iranian Cultural Attaché. Lock tried to persuade Oan that this would not be helpful and offered to speak to the police. Oan agreed: 'But no tricks or I will kill the hostages.' Lock then proceeded by calling from the open window on the first floor: 'There is a hostage about to be killed unless you allow Oan full use of telephone and telex.' When this was refused, Oan pressed the gun harder into the side of Ezzatti's head, before pushing him away. 'I want to talk to a man from your BBC, a man who knows Harris', Oan demanded. 'I set a new deadline in a few hours.'

At last, at 1500hrs, the police brought in Tony Crabb, the managing editor of BBC TV News and a personal friend of Sim Harris. Crabb listened as Harris shouted the terrorists' demands from the first-floor window, taking down the information in a notebook: a coach to convey the gunmen, hostages and one Arab ambassador to Heathrow; the non-Iranian hostages to be released at Heathrow; and an aircraft to take the remaining hostages, gunmen and ambassador to an unspecified country in the Middle East (presumably Iraq) where all the remaining hostages would be released. Oan also insisted that his grievances were to be broadcast by the BBC that evening.

Meanwhile, after a lengthy search the police tracked down the embassy caretaker, who was on holiday. He had an intimate knowledge of the embassy layout and supplied invaluable information to the authorities, not least over the question that most vexed the SAS: whether the ground-floor and first-floor

MAY 2
1980

1500hrs:
Terrorists issue their demands to the BBC's Tony Crabb

MAY 2
1980

2030hrs:
The embassy caretaker briefs the SAS and police on the interior of the building

windows were armour-plated. They were. He also revealed that behind the wooden door at the front of the embassy was an ornate steel security door. The caretaker proved a mine of information, knowing the location not only of the major rooms but also of virtually every storeroom and broom cupboard. Everyone in the briefing room listened intently, keenly aware that his knowledge could save them from potential disaster, not least because one plan had involved emerging at a run from next door, no. 14, armed with sledgehammers, and battering in the ground-floor windows and main door of the embassy. Had they proceeded with this plan, the armour plating would have entirely confounded the assault and given time for the terrorists to kill the hostages. As a result of this new intelligence, revised plans had to be laid, orders rewritten, the assault teams rebriefed and appropriate demolition equipment issued.

By late evening, Oan was furious. He had spent the evening listening to news bulletins on BBC radio, his aggravation and frustration growing as each successive report failed to broadcast his aims and grievances accurately. They had stated his new demands in brief terms, but to Oan's disbelief and anger they had misreported them. Whereas the terrorists wanted the Arab negotiators to conduct talks through the British government, the BBC stated that negotiations were to be conducted between the ambassadors and Iranian officials. The evening therefore closed on an increasingly tense basis.

Day Four: Saturday, 3 May

At 0605hrs, the field telephone rang at Alpha Control, where the duty negotiator answered the phone politely, only to be cut off in mid-sentence by the enraged Oan. 'You are liars!' he declared. 'You have cheated and deceived me over my demands.' The police negotiator sought to deflect this by remaining calm and changing the subject, enquiring into what was wanted for breakfast. Oan was not to be put off, and demanded to speak to an Arab ambassador, only to be told that the authorities were doing their best. The Foreign Office was arranging talks with Jordanian, Kuwaiti and Syrian diplomats in the hope of breaking the deadlock – but that this would take time – a standard delaying tactic employed by police in a stand-off. Clearly the government was unwilling to meet the terrorists' demands for mediation and safe conduct out of the country. Oan recognized this as deceit, informed the police that the British hostages would be the last to be released and demanded the reappearance of Tony Crabb, barring which a hostage would be killed. He hung up the phone, leaving the police to make the next move.

Crabb finally arrived at 1530. Harris strongly reprimanded him for delaying the broadcast of the terrorists' demands and for failing to ensure that the statement was absolutely correct. The police negotiator, standing near Crabb, then intervened, agreeing to take down Oan's statement and vouch for its accuracy before transmission. With a notebook and pencil in hand, he transcribed Oan's words as shouted down from the first-floor window by Mustapha Karkouti. Oan was taking no chances: he demanded a guarantee that the BBC release the statement with perfect accuracy and on the next news bulletin. But by conceding to this, the terrorists were providing the police with a bargaining chip. Accordingly, the negotiator asked for a show of good faith on the part of the gunmen: some hostages had to be released in exchange. Oan paused before replying. 'We give you one,' he declared, but the negotiator required more. Another minute passed with tensions high. 'I give you two,' came the reply, and with that the bargain was concluded. A short time later, two hostages were selected for release: first, Ali Guil Ghanzafar, a

Pakistani teacher, whose release appears to have been made solely on the basis of his loud snoring, which had kept everyone awake. The second hostage was Hiyech Kanji, a pregnant woman. The exchange was not straightforward, however, for Oan demanded that his statement be broadcast, exactly as conveyed, before the release of the two hostages. The police would not have it; the hostages must be released first. Deadlock ensued.

Receiving the police demand by phone, Oan angrily threw the receiver to the floor, threatening to kill a hostage at 2100hrs if the BBC failed to release the statement on the nine o'clock news. Karkouti, who had had enough, fell to his knees and begged Oan not to kill a hostage. To what extent this influenced his subsequent behaviour will never be known, but Oan decided on a compromise, releasing the pregnant woman before the 2100hrs deadline. The statement was duly read on the news, just as Oan had dictated it, by the Head of Information at Scotland Yard, to the overwhelming relief of the hostages and the jubilation of the gunmen. Soon Ali-Gholi Ghazan-Far was taken down to the ground floor, walked out of the embassy's front door and crossed the road to a waiting ambulance.

Every hostage released was welcome news to the authorities, but SAS plans continued apace on the basis that an assault might still be required. At 2300hrs, therefore, with the sky clear and star-filled, an SAS team gingerly moved across the rooftops towards 16 Princes Gate. Traffic was quiet in Knightsbridge and South Kensington, with tourists and those who would normally be going to dinner or a pub conspicuously absent from the cordoned streets. But the silence was suddenly broken when one of the SAS men broke a slate with his foot, giving the impression that a pistol shot had been fired. The soldier pointed to his foot, the mistake was understood, and the team gave the thumbs-up to the police sniper concealed on the roof of no. 14, before moving on.

The team carefully made its way across the rooftops, avoiding the forest of aerials and telescopic poles, wires and satellite dishes. The reconnaissance leader then discovered it: moonlight reflecting on glass – the embassy skylight. The word was passed at a whisper, and the recce leader knelt down to discover if the skylight was locked. It was. Another member of the team then proposed peeling back the strip of lead waterproofing positioned around the edge of the glass. Careful work for a quarter of an hour offered success: one of the team was able to lift one of the glass panes from the frame, enabling him to reach through the gap and remove the lock. He gradually eased open the skylight. As SAS trooper Pete Winner recalled,

> Moonlight immediately flooded the small room beneath us. We found ourselves looking down into a cramped bathroom. Directly below us was a large white enamel bath. In the left-hand corner was a grimy wash-basin, and opposite it was the door that could lead us to the top landing of the Embassy and eventually to the terrorist stronghold. I felt a sudden rush of excitement, a surge of adrenalin, at the thought of the options this new development offered. I had to stifle an urge to become the first SAS man into the Embassy. It would have been quite easy to grip the wooden surround of the skylight base and lower myself down on to the edge of the bath. But thoughts of immortality were interrupted by a hand on my shoulder and by Roy's voice whispering, 'Come on. Let's get back to the holding area. We can tell the boss we've got a guaranteed entry point.

On the rear rooftop of no. 16 the team also secured abseil ropes to the several chimneys so that a rapid descent could be made down the rear of the building to the lower floors for entry through the windows.

Lieutenant-Colonel Mike Rose, Commander, 22 SAS. Rose was operational commander on the ground at Princes Gate, responsible for drawing up military plans and advising Brigadier Peter de la Billière, Director of SAS Group, which includes all the Regiment's units.

Day Five: Sunday, 4 May

By the evening, the terrorists appeared to be in better spirits than before, for news bulletins were reporting that Arab ambassadors had agreed to meet with British government officials to discuss the situation with a view to negotiating an end to the crisis. Oan was delighted at this, and now wanted only one Arab ambassador to negotiate safe passage for his men. He also agreed to release Mustapha Karkouti, who was now feverish. At 2000hrs the journalist walked free through the main entrance of the embassy. Some speculation has arisen since the siege that the police doctored the food to induce illness. According to de la Billière, Dellow did consult a doctor about its viability, but eventually rejected the idea as 'impracticable'. Nevertheless, as before, the release of a hostage provided further intelligence to the police, who were now certain of the number of terrorists involved and the types of weapons they carried. What remained a mystery, however, was whether or not they had laid explosives to blow up the building, as they had claimed.

By this time, the SAS had formulated their assault plan, should it be required, in such a way that simultaneous entry could be achieved at various points, with clearly defined demarcation of responsibility to reduce the risk of soldiers firing on one another and the delays gave them the opportunity to practise the scenario in the mock-up rooms laid out at Regent's Park Barracks. At the same time, COBR's lengthy discussions continued in earnest, with all options considered. When opportunity arose, de la Billière, dressed as a civilian and unknown at the time to the press and public (recognition coming during the Gulf War in 1991, when he would lead British forces) returned to Princes Gate to reconnoitre and consult with Mike Rose, whom he found 'irrepressibly optimistic' and worked exceptionally well with John Dellow, to the extent that they had established a system of co-ordinated intelligence-gathering between the SAS and the police, and were briefing one another every six hours.

These discussions culminated that evening with dinner and a meeting at de la Billière's flat, including Rose and Major Hector Gullan, commander of the assault team. De la Billière recalled how the three 'spread out large-scale drawings of the Embassy on the floor, and... examined every detail. It was a typical SAS occasion: not a formal briefing, but an opportunity for people who knew each other extremely well to exchange ideas and further refine what was already a clearly thought out operation.'

Day Six: Monday, 5 May

Negotiations with the terrorists continued by telephone, but the government refused to make concessions, and with no Arab mediators supplied in accordance with the terrorists' demands, the atmosphere in the embassy grew more tense. The police had only a modicum of bargaining power left and were losing what little confidence the terrorists had in them. The male hostages, assembled on the second floor in room 9, were awakened at 0630hrs. Oan told Lock that he had heard strange noises in the night and was certain the police had managed to infiltrate the building. Oddly, rather than searching the building himself, Oan ordered Lock to do so. Sim Harris and Ron Morris, meanwhile, began their usual routine of washing the cups from the previous evening and preparing the simple breakfast of biscuits and tea, which Morris passed round to the women in room 9A. Lock returned from his investigation of the building to report that there was no one to be found.

Circumstances appeared to be looking up, for some progress had been made. At 1000hrs, however, the arrival of a telegram from Tehran, addressed to the hostages, changed this. It was from the Iranian Foreign Minister, and declared that his nation was proud of the 'steadfastness and forbearance' of the hostages during a difficult time, yet implicitly consigned them to death with the words: 'We feel certain that you are all ready for martyrdom alongside your nation.' Tension rose significantly at 1100hrs when Oan discovered a bulge in the first-floor landing wall which separated the Iranian Embassy from the Ethiopian Embassy next door. He led Lock to see the evidence, demanding an explanation and expressing strong suspicion that this was to serve as an entry point for the police. Lock failed to assuage him, with Oan declaring, 'Your police, they are up to something, I am convinced. I'm going to make new arrangements for the hostages.' He stormed off upstairs to the second floor with a view to moving the hostages. The degree of agitation was now evident in the faces and body movements of the gunmen. Their weapons were poised at the ready, and they began to move the male hostages from room 9 along the corridor to room 10, the telex room. Things were clearly deteriorating, and at midday Lock, now exhausted, sought further methods for pacifying the gunmen, suggesting to Oan that together they speak to the police negotiator. Oan was prepared to give Lock five minutes with the police.

Lock and Harris went to the first-floor balcony and began communication with the police negotiator. 'Now listen to me', Harris said earnestly. 'Lives are at risk, time is running out.' The negotiator calmly declared that they were doing everything possible. Harris was insistent, claiming the Foreign Office was not doing its job. 'It all takes time', replied the negotiator. Harris observed that time was running out and demanded to know the whereabouts of the Arab ambassador requested to mediate. 'Things are moving along as quickly as possible', came the negotiator's reply. 'The Foreign Office are still in discussion with the ambassadors, and if you listen to the BBC World Service you will get your confirmation.'

At 1300hrs a BBC news bulletin announced that the meeting between COBR and the Arab ambassadors was still under way – in fact, no such meeting took place – and that no final decision about who would mediate had yet been reached. Oan, outraged at this news, picked up the telephone that put him into immediate contact with the police negotiator. He was in deadly earnest now: 'You have run out of time. There will be no more talking. Bring the ambassador to the phone or I will kill a hostage in forty-five minutes.' For the next 40 minutes Alpha Control heard no further word from the gunmen. Then, at 1340hrs, the telephone buzzer sounded, whereupon the negotiator answered it with a calm voice. 'Hello, it's Stuart here.' Lock then spoke. 'Stuart, they have a hostage and they are going to kill him. They have him at the bottom of the stairs. Something terrible is going to happen. They are tying his hands behind his back. They are tying him to the banister.' Oan then came on the line with a threatening tone: 'If you don't accept my demand, I will shoot him.' The police negotiator urged him not to take any action that was 'counterproductive'. Oan would have none of it. 'I told you, I have waited long enough. You have deceived me. Someone will die.'

The hostage was Abbas Lavasani, the Chief Press Officer and a zealous supporter of his government, who over the course of the siege had provoked the gunmen several times, not least over the anti-Khomeini graffiti that the terrorists had written on the walls, and had offered to die as a martyr to the Islamic Revolution. A minute passed before communication resumed. A highly nervous, gasping voice then spoke. 'I am one of the hostages. My name is Lavasani.' There followed another pause. Another voice, agitated, interrupted him. 'No names. No names.' Immediately thereafter, at 1345hrs, came a series of ominous cracks that sounded distinctly like three shots.

MAY 3 1980

1530hrs: Terrorists issue revised demands to Tony Crabb

MAY 3 1980

2100hrs: BBC broadcasts the terrorists' full demands on television and radio

MAY 4 1980

2000hrs: Terrorists release Mustapha Karkouti

Troopers of the Reserve Team covering the rear of the embassy. The Reserve Signaller stands at right while on his left, a Reserve Trooper, kneeling, carries an MP5 sub-machine gun fitted with a silencer.

The SAS team, still poised next door, heard the shots, too. Peter Winner immediately appreciated that an assault was inevitable:

I reached for my MP5, removed the magazine, cocked the action and caught the ejected 9-milly round. I then stripped the weapon and began to clean the working parts meticulously. This is it, I thought as I lightly oiled the breech-block. There could be no going back now. A hostage had been murdered. Direct action would have to be taken. As I threaded the metal beads of the Heckler Koch pull-through down the barrel of the machine pistol, I let my mind wander through the problems of attacking a building with over fifty rooms. We would need speed, we would need surprise, we would need aggression.

The line was still open, and the police asked Lock what had happened; he did not know. Both Rose and Dellow believed that the shots were not a bluff – that someone had been killed. De la Billière immediately made his way back to Whitehall to report to COBR. The Home Secretary was not in fact there, but rather at his official residence, Dorneywood, near Slough, about to sit down to a lunch that, with the siege in deadlock, had not been cancelled. The shots had now changed everything, and Whitelaw, accompanied by his Private Secretary, John Chilcot, agreed that he was immediately required back in London, which he reached, with the aid of police outriders to clear his 20-mile path from Slough to Whitehall, in an astonishing 19 minutes. Whitelaw later recalled in his memoirs: 'I did once look at the speedometer [of his Jaguar] as we were going over Hammersmith Broadway and noticed that it showed well over a hundred. The assembled company at the Cabinet Office was obviously amazed to see us so soon. But there was no time for such customary comments as, "You have been quick." We had serious business on hand.'

In the Cabinet Office Briefing Room, de la Billière discovered a new sense of urgency:

> If one of the hostages *had* been executed, the murder moved things sharply forward, and a military operation looked probable. For the next two hours, together with Whitelaw and Boorman, I went through every detail of the options and risks involved. I explained that, with the progressive refinement of our plan, the risks had steadily diminished, but nevertheless were still high. I said that even if things went well, we must expect forty per cent of the people in the building to become casualties. Anything less than that would be a very good outcome. At the end I reiterated that the decision to go in would be a political one, even though it led to the use of military force.

The Home Secretary told de la Billière that if the operations went ahead he would not interfere, and that if it failed he would accept full responsibility for the outcome. De la Billière was to put his men on standby, ready to attack at short notice. He passed the word to Rose, who in turn informed Dellow that the two teams would need two hours to be ready to carry out the now finely honed plan of assault. At 1550hrs Rose therefore began to prepare, and by 1630hrs de la Billière was back at Princes Gate, examining the area one final time to ensure the accuracy of his thoughts on the plan, and to enable him to describe the area to those not on the scene. He then went to visit the troops awaiting the signal to move in:

> In the Forward Holding Area I talked to members of the assault team, and found the atmosphere typical of the SAS immediately before an operation: there was no sense of over-excitement or tension; rather, an air of professionalism and quiet confidence prevailed. These men had been superbly trained, and they had so often practised the kind of task they were about to carry out that it had become almost an everyday event. This is not to say that they lacked courage or imagination: on the contrary, they knew full well that the terrorists were heavily armed, and that the building could be wired with explosives, and might go up as they broke in. They simply accepted the risks and carried on.

At 1700hrs Rose informed Dellow that his men were ready to assault the embassy with ten minutes' notice. Shortly thereafter Lock reported that the terrorists were threatening to kill several hostages, and were moving furniture to barricade doors and windows. At 1820hrs, the police suspecting that there was very little time left – that events were reaching a crisis point – then produced the Imam from the mosque in Regent's Street and put him on the phone to Oan. In the course of their conversation, three more shots were heard in the embassy, upon which Oan said that a hostage had been killed, with the rest to die in 30 minutes. The threat did not appear to be a bluff, for shortly after the shots had occurred, the front door of the embassy was opened and Lavasani's body was dumped on the steps outside the building.

The terrorists got on the line to Alpha Control, ordering the police to collect the body and warning of another killing in 45 minutes. Two police officers quickly carried the body away on a stretcher and an immediate autopsy revealed that

Lavasani had been dead for more than an hour, and thus could not have been killed by the three recently fired shots. This suggested that Lavasani was in fact the second hostage to be killed; an unidentified victim having been slain at the time of the shots fired earlier in the afternoon. In fact, only Lavasani had been killed, but Whitelaw recorded in his diary how the production of Lavasani's body appeared to confirm in the minds of observers that in fact two hostages had been murdered. Be that as it may, Lavasani's death sealed the terrorists' fate, for police cease to negotiate any further once a hostage has been killed, except to stall while an assault is prepared.

With one hostage confirmed dead and a second presumed so, Sir David McNee, Commissioner of the Metropolitan Police, telephoned COBR to request permission to hand control over to the SAS. The secret line failed to function, but on an open one McNee told Whitelaw that the police could do nothing more: it was time for the SAS to do the job. As Whitelaw relates:

> It was a particularly strained moment for both of us, for we appreciated the risk of sending in the SAS to storm the building. And of course we had in mind that PC Trevor Lock was among the hostages and at grave risk. However, I had discussed the pros and cons of such a decision exhaustively with my team and I was in no doubt what I had to do.

Whitelaw, in turn contacted the Prime Minister for her approval. Thatcher related this period in her memoirs:

> I was called back early from Chequers [the Prime Minister's official country residence] and we were driving back to London when a further message came over the car-phone… Apparently, the information was that the hostages' lives were now at risk. Willie [Whitelaw] wanted my permission to send in the SAS. 'Yes, go in,' I said. The car pulled back out onto the road, while I tried to visualize what was happening and waited for the outcome.

Whitelaw then contacted Dellow, giving him authority to hand control over to Rose. De la Billière, in turn, phoned Rose to authorize him to accept responsibility and proceed to initiate the plan. The chain of command having been scrupulously observed, at 1907hrs precisely Dellow passed formal control of the situation over to Rose to implement his rescue plan at his discretion. De la Billière recalled events thus:

> Mike [Rose] very properly insisted that he must have written authority for the assault (in case someone should later claim that he had exceeded his brief), and Dellow was on the point of signing the document a couple of minutes before seven o'clock when another telephone call suggested that the hostages might after all be released. A delay ensued while the interpreter tried to work out what had been said; but the message was so muddled that no sense could be made of it, and Dellow signed the authority at 1907. So, although he himself retained overall command, control of the military assault passed to Rose.

The Ministry of Defence was now constitutionally in charge of the area around the embassy. 'At that moment of decision,' Whitelaw recalled, 'I felt very lonely and yet strangely calm. Curiously, I do not remember contemplating the appalling possibilities which might result. I suppose this was because I knew that there really was no alternative.' There then followed ten extremely tense minutes while the SAS men made final preparations and got into position. During this period, the police made

MAY 5
1980

1550hrs:
SAS asked to prepare for an assault

MAY 5
19804

1700hrs:
Assault teams are in place and ready to go

every effort to occupy Oan, to prevent him killing any further hostages, to distract him while the troops got into position for the assault and to fix Oan's position in the embassy, for the field telephone was believed to be on the first floor. Dellow now ordered his negotiators to alter their tactics entirely: to prevaricate by offering various concessions – coaches to take everyone to Heathrow, enquiries about the number required, arrangements about where they were to park outside the embassy, who was to drive them and promises that the Iraqi ambassador was on his way to the scene. Speaking in turn, two negotiators kept Oan occupied, though on several occasions he angrily handed the receiver to Lock, who anxiously demanded reassurance that no assault was imminent. While the police continued to spin out the conversation, two four-man teams were moving along the roof, placing their abseil ropes and lowering stun-charges down the light-well. Others were making their way gingerly along the sunken alleyways at the front and rear of the embassy. Snipers, meanwhile, hidden in trees and buildings around the embassy, waited for an opportunity to assist the coming assault.

De la Billière, still in the Cabinet Office Briefing Room, described the rising tension there:

> Until then the room had always been filled by a buzz of discussion, as ideas were put up, knocked about and adopted or discarded. Now there was nothing more that anyone could do or say. The SAS were going in, to resolve the situation or fail. The talk died

Two officers of the Metropolitan Police (one crouching) acting as stretcher-bearers, carrying away the body of Abbas Lavasani whom Salim had executed. The officer covering his colleagues with a rifle is from D11, the Met's Firearms Team. From this point the only option open to the terrorists was surrender or to face an assault. An autopsy conducted immediately after the recovery of the body revealed that Lavasani had been dead for some hours, and therefore was not the victim of the shooting heard around 1900hrs on 1 May.

away until no sound remained except that of the digital clock on the end wall. *Snap!* went the little flap as it fell, marking the passage of every minute. *Snap… Snap…*

MAY 5
1980

1802hrs:
Terrorists shoot
Abbas Lavasani and
throw his body into
the street

Oddly, those assembled did not switch on the television monitors in the room to watch live what millions of viewers around the world were about to witness. As such, de la Billière, wearing headphones, was the only person in the room in direct contact with events at Princes Gate, and thus was poised to give a running commentary based on orders he could hear being transmitted by Gullan, as well as the sound of the men talking to each other as they moved into their respective positions.

There were at this time 20 hostages in the embassy, 15 of whom, all men, were in room 10, the telex room on the second floor overlooking the street. They had been moved there a few hours before, once the terrorists had suspected that an assault was imminent. These hostages were being guarded by three terrorists, some of whom had been moving on an irregular basis to check other rooms. Meanwhile, five female hostages, all members of the embassy staff, were being guarded by one terrorist in room 9 on the opposite side of the building, across a landing. Oan, of course, was on the telephone, which the authorities still believed to be on the first-floor landing. It was known that at the front of the embassy the only feasible method of entry was through the windows on the first-floor balcony. These windows were, however, made of armour-plated glass, which would have to be blown out with an explosive charge. With the murder of Lavasani, the terrorists – notwithstanding continued negotiations with the police – could logically assume that an assault might be launched, therefore denying the SAS the element of complete surprise. As such, it was critically important that the SAS assaults, both at the front and rear of the embassy, be executed simultaneously.

Red Team was assembled on the roof, the plan being to use two four-man teams: one to abseil down to the second-floor balcony at the back of the building, with the other assaulting the third floor, while more men would blow in the skylight

'B' Squadron Command Group situated at the back of the embassy. The Squadron Sergeant-Major (back left) holds the earpiece of his radio, a respirator secured to his arm, with the Intelligence Officer beside him. Standing in the foreground from left to right are 'Pronto', the Signals Officer; the Squadron OC's Signaller, wearing a gas mask; the Squadron OC, codenamed 'Lysander', wearing a camouflage jacket; and a member of the Reserve Team, a torch fastened to his jacket.

on the fourth floor to enter the building by that means. Blue Team was assigned the task of clearing the ground floor, basement and first floor.

A member of the assault team described the plan of action thus:

When we had arrived at the start of the siege, we had been told to be ready to storm the building within 15 minutes. This would mean going in using firearms, stun grenades and CS gas and trying to reach the hostages before they were killed. At that stage we had no idea of the hostages' whereabouts. I looked at the embassy and thought of clearing 50 rooms one by one, while all the time looking out for the terrorists and their prisoners. F***ing nightmare.

However, because the negotiators did their stuff, we were given a few days in which to prepare a more comprehensive plan, and we spent the time familiarising ourselves with every part of the building. The plan, like most good ones, was fairly simple: "Red Team" would enter and tackle the top half of the building, while "Blue Team" would clear the lower half of the embassy. We would also have the support of a multitude of snipers, which gave me, for one, a reassuring feeling. (Crawford, *The SAS at Close Quarters*, p. 71)

De la Billière described the plan, which had been perfected over the course of several days, thus:

The essence of it was speed and surprise: the aim was to attack every floor of the building simultaneously, and to break in so fast on all levels that the gunmen would not

**MAY 5
1980**

**1907hrs:
Operational control of
the situation handed
over to the SAS**

The abseil team minutes before the radio instruction, 'Standby. Standby. Go!' They are attaching the abseil ropes to their body harnesses prior to taking up positions for the descent onto the second floor balcony.

The abseil team, now fully rigged up, awaiting the order to begin their descent down the back of the building onto the second-floor balcony.

have time to execute anyone. Success depended on every SAS man knowing his task precisely: the soldiers had to be able to pick out the terrorists, recognize every hostage (from memorizing photographs), and keep within pre-set boundaries so that there was no risk of shooting each other.

The start of the raid would be signalled by the explosion of a pair of stun charges. These were to be placed on a glass dome which was situated in the middle of the building on top of the second floor. Initially it had been considered as an entry point but the planners realized that a loud explosion at the centre of the building would distract the hostage-takers just as the SAS abseiled down the sides of the building.

THE SAS ASSAULT

At 1923 hours, over the assault teams' radios came the codeword 'Hyde Park' – the signal for the abseilers to hitch themselves to their ropes; then, a few moments later, 'London Bridge' – the signal to descend – followed by Gullan's shout of 'Go! Go! Go!' Operation *Nimrod*, the codename for the SAS rescue, was now operational. But a problem immediately arose: the police negotiators were still on the phone with Oan, who interrupted the call to say that he suspected foul play. He had heard a suspicious sound and, despite reassurances from the police that all was well, put down the receiver to investigate. The assault began with a diversionary explosion that tore through the skylight on the third floor, meant to coincide with the signal for Red Team to abseil from the roof while Blue Team, working simultaneously, executed an entry through the library at the rear of the ground floor. In the event, the operations conducted by the two teams were not begun absolutely simultaneously. As de la Billière recalled:

> I heard the detonation through my headphones – or rather, I heard two. I knew at once that something had gone wrong. The explosions – the stun charges in the light-well, and the windows being blown in [at the front of the embassy] had become separated by a few seconds. Or had the whole building gone up? It was a bad moment. I went back into the Briefing Room and said, 'I'm afraid there have been two explosions. It may be that our people have failed to coordinate, or the terrorists may have blown up the Embassy, and our soldiers with it.

The sequence of events that followed is best understood by dividing them between the two teams, Red and Blue, and then sub-dividing them by area of responsibility into the five four-man teams deployed.

Red Team (Team 1): Third and fourth floors

Team 1 from Red Team blew in the glass dome in the stairwell leading to the second floor, entered the building and proceeded to run upstairs to clear the 3rd and 4th floors.

The team with call sign Zero Delta stand in front of the embassy behind the high wall which runs along the edge of the embassy car park. They have just fired CS gas grenades through the front windows of the building and are now covering its front with their Brownings.

Previous pages

Dressed entirely in black
from their balaclava helmets
to their gloves and boots,
assault teams make a
forcible entry into the rear
of the embassy. Those on
the second-floor balcony
reached this position via
abseil ropes secured from
the roof. While abseiling
is used in descending a
rock face during mountain
training or operations, in
its counter-terrorist role it is
used to descend the face of
a building, usually from the
roof, to permit access
through a window. The
assault team on the ground
floor wield a 'hooligan bar',
a metre-long steel tool
designed specifically for
breaking windows and,
with its attachments and
hooks, pulling away the
debris or, in the case of
sash windows, as a sort
of grappling hook to aid
in climbing through
the opening made.
An adjustable strap is
also fitted, securing it
to the back of the wrist.

Red Team (Team 2): Second floor (rear entry)

Team 2, which was positioned on the roof, began their descent on two abseil ropes down the rear of the building on to the second-floor balcony. As one member of the assault team later recalled:

> We were on the roof waiting for the order to go. We had all made our last-minute checks – respirators, weapons, assault suits and stun grenades – and now we wanted to be off. The adrenalin rush was unbelievable. The word was given and we started to descend from the roof. I fed the rope through my descender as we moved quickly and silently down the side of the rear of the building. Then, disaster. The boss [a Fijian staff sergeant] got snagged in his harness. Some of the lads tried to help him, but then one of them accidentally broke a window with his foot. S***! (Crawford, *The SAS at Close Quarters*, pp. 71–72)

The broken glass alerted Oan, who was still on the telephone with the police negotiator. He put down the receiver and went to investigate, followed by PC Lock. The first abseil team at the rear was to have awaited the sound of the explosion created by their comrades at the front of the building before beginning their own entry into the embassy. This was now impossible; they had to go now. All hell broke as snipers fired CS gas into the embassy as the SAS attempted to gain entry.

Meanwhile, the Red Team leader remained entangled in his rope, possibly the result of defective nylon, which could overheat as a result of friction, causing it to ravel into a knot and prevent the abseiler from descending further. The team was to have used explosive charges to gain access through the windows, but with their leader suspended above the second-floor windows this was impossible. They did, however, throw exploding stun grenades and CS gas canisters into the embassy. These appear to have been responsible for setting fire to newspapers, sprinkled with lighter fuel, which the terrorists had laid under the windows, beneath heavy drape curtains, which began to burn him through the broken windows as he hung suspended. He avoided serious injury as best he could, however, by kicking the outside wall and swinging himself away. A subsequent wave of abseilers, seeing his predicament, cut him loose, leaving him to crash down on to the balcony. Despite his serious burns, he entered the building with the rest of his team.

Pete Scholey, an SAS trooper himself, though not present on the day, explains Sergeant Tommy Palmer's experience of the attack at this point:

> When Tommy went in through this balcony window the curtains were a mass of flames and his respirator and hood caught light. He thought his burning kit was about to turn him into a human candle, but he quickly ducked back out of the window, ripped off the smouldering gear and dived back in again, bareheaded. He now had no protection against the CS gas that was billowing through the building, he had scorch burns to his head and neck and was slapping at his singed hair with one hand to make sure it wasn't still burning. Not that he had much time to worry about that. One of the terrorists was crouched at the opposite side of the elegant room trying to set light to a beautiful floor carpet that had been splashed with kerosene. If he'd waited a couple of minutes, the flames devouring the room from Tommy's end would have done the job for him. Tommy didn't wait. As soon as his feet touched the floor he had his MP5 levelled at the terrorist and squeezed the trigger. Nothing happened. A two-second burst would have been enough to empty most of the 30-round magazine into the man, but nothing happened. All Tommy got was the 'dead man's click' – a stoppage. The terrorist froze for a heartbeat, staring down the barrel of Tommy's gun. Tommy dropped the MP5 and

snatched his 9mm Browning from the quick-draw holster strapped to this thigh. In the split second he took to do that, the terrorist recovered his senses and took to his heels. He dashed through the door into the corridor as Tommy sprinted across the room, the kerosene in the carpet squelching under his boots.

Blinking to clear his eyes of the stinging tear gas and acrid smoke from the blazing room, Tommy pounded out into the corridor. Straight away he spotted the back of the terrorist's shirt, the man racing away from him down the hallway. In his hand, the terrorist now held what Tommy immediately recognized as a Russian fragmentation grenade. The man was heading for a room that Tommy knew was full of hostages. Two more running steps and then he took aim as the man paused for an instant outside the room. That instant was long enough for Tommy to shoot him in the head and the man dropped to the floor. (Scholey, *SAS Heroes*, pp. 218–219)

Two members of the abseil team seconds after receiving the order to descend. They have reached the second-floor balcony windows, through which they intend to enter the building.

Meanwhile, in the telex room, three terrorists had begun firing on the hostages. For the SAS men there was no time to be lost, for they could hear both the shots and the screams of the hostages. In a wild hail of gunfire one of the terrorists shot the assistant press attaché, Ali Akbar Samadzadeh in the chest, killing him instantly. Sitting beside him on the floor was the chargé d'affaires, Dr Gholam-Ali Afrouz, who, first shot in the face and wounded, was shot again in the legs as he lay on the floor. Another hostage, Ahmed Dadgar, the medical aide, sitting on the opposite side of Afrouz, was shot in the chest, though, like Afrouz, subsequently recovered. A fourth hostage, the embassy doorman, Abbas Fallahi, was also caught in the gunman's fire, but a fifty-pence coin in his pocket fortuitously saved his life. From the back office, meanwhile, the rest of Red Team, including Tommy Palmer, rushed for the telex room where the terrorists now sought to mingle amongst the hostages to try to save themselves.

According to Morris, the embassy chauffeur and the only British hostage in the room, the terrorists did not put up their hands, place them on their heads or show any other sign of an intention to surrender. As the soldiers burst into the room they demanded that the hostages identify the terrorists. One of them pointed at a terrorist who held a grenade in his hands and was shot instantly with a well-aimed shot to the head. Other hostages mixed themselves in among the hostages in the general chaos. Another terrorist was identified, pulled out of line and made to lie on the floor. However, he made some suspicious movements and was instantly shot. When his body was turned over the SAS troopers found a Soviet grenade in his hand.

Two terrorists were killed in the telex room, but a third remained hidden among the hostages. Once the telex room was secure, the team moved on, forcing their way into other rooms and efficiently clearing them. In each case they followed the same routine – shooting off the lock, kicking in the door, throwing in a stun grenade and then clearing it. It was becoming increasingly difficult to see as the building became filled with smoke and CS gas. Nonetheless, the four female hostages held together in the cipher room were successfully freed and led downstairs, together with the hostages from the telex room, among whom was hiding a yet undiscovered terrorist.

Blue Team (Team 3): First floor front

While Red Team was busy entering from the rear second and upper floors, Team 3 of Blue Team was seeking entry through the front of the embassy via the first-floor balcony of an adjacent building, where a two-man section moved across to the balcony, placing special frame charges of plastic explosives against the window while the other man of the section provided cover. The large rectangles of plastic explosive were placed flush against the glass, so that an entire window was blown in when the charges were detonated. They discovered, however, that Sim Harris was too close to the window, upon which they yelled for him to lie down, which he did. After the fuse was activated, the second man gave a hand signal to his comrades below, and both men rushed for cover to the adjoining balcony by clambering across a short alloy ladder laid horizontally between the two structures. A tremendous explosion followed detonation, but by that time two minutes had already passed since the men at the rear had begun their abseil descent.

With the armoured glass shattered in the impressive blast, the way was now clear: the SAS men threw in flash-bang grenades and then entered the first floor before the

SAS men scrambling for cover after placing the frame charge.

The siege reaches its climax: SAS men await the detonation of the frame charge before entering the embassy. The SAS, hitherto almost completely unknown to the public, would make its dramatic public debut in full view of millions of television viewers, most of whom were home for Bank Holiday Monday.

smoke had cleared and the building had stopped shuddering from the explosion. As a member of Blue Team recalled:

> Then we were in. We threw in stun grenades and then quickly followed. There was a thundering bang and a blinding flash as the stun grenades went off. Designed to disorientate any hostiles who were in the room, they were a godsend. No one in here, good. I looked round, the stun grenades had set light to the curtains, not so good. No time to stop and put out the fire. Keep moving. We swept the room, then heard shouts coming from another office. We hurried towards the noise, and burst in to see one of the terrorists struggling with the copper who had been on duty when the embassy had been seized: PC Lock. (Crawford, *The SAS at Close Quarters*, p. 74)

The terrorist in question was in fact their leader, Oan, who, on seeing one of the SAS men coming through the back of the building, was rugby-tackled by Trevor Lock.

MAY 5 1980

1923hrs: The assault begins

Two members of the front balcony assault team, having placed the frame charge ready to blow in the front window, retiring to a safe distance. Seconds later the massive explosion almost caught the last man. Smoke and debris from the explosions, combined with the CS gas shot through the windows, make the scene a potentially confusing one. It was the job of the SAS to look beyond such hazards and distractions and seek out the terrorists before they killed any other hostages.

An image taken immediately after the spectacular explosion that blew in the window on the front first-floor balcony. The team leader has just thrown a 'flash-bang' stun grenade through the broken window. Seconds after this photo was taken the team followed the grenade into the room and killed Salim, the terrorist leader.

In the course of the confused struggle between them, Lock drew the .38 revolver he had been concealing since the beginning of the siege. The SAS man shouted for Lock to move away, whereupon Oan pointed his weapon at Lock and prepared to fire. The unnamed SAS member continues his account:

> One of the lads rushed forward and got Lock away, then pumped a long burst from his MP5 into the terrorist. The bullets hit his head and chest, sending his lifeless body sprawling against the wall. One down, five to go.

> Lock was bundled out and we continued our search. The building was filling with CS gas and smoke. We had to free the hostages and get out as quickly as possible. Where the f*** were they? (Crawford, *The SAS at Close Quarters*, p. 74)

Blue Team: Entry on ground floor (rear); clearing ground floor and stairs (Team 4) and cellar (Team 5)

Next door, at no. 14, Pete Winner's troop, in Team No. 5, heard the order screamed through their earpieces. Pushing open the french windows at the rear of no. 14, and moving towards the rear of no. 16, he caught sight of the snipers positioned in a block of flats to his left. His team was meant to use explosive charges to blow in the rear french doors, but this was found to be impossible. He relates the story thus:

> We took up a position behind a low wall as a demolition call sign ran forward and placed the explosive charge on the Embassy french windows. It was then that we saw the abseiler swinging in the flames on the first floor [sic: second]. It was all noise, confusion, bursts of sub-machine gun fire. I could hear women screaming. Christ! It's all going wrong, I thought. There's no way we can blow that charge without injuring the abseiler. Instant change of plans. The sledge-man ran forward and lifted the sledge-hammer. One blow, just above the lock, was sufficient to open the door. They say luck shines on the brave. We were certainly lucky. If that door had been bolted or barricaded, we would have had big problems.

> 'Go. Go. Go. Get in at the rear.' The voice was screaming in my ear. The eight call signs rose to their feet as one and then we were sweeping in through the splintered door. All

Opposite

The last two members of the four-man, front balcony assault team, about to enter the building to clear the first floor. Salim, the terrorist leader, is only seconds away from death. The raid on the Iranian Embassy brought the SAS, a hitherto virtually unknown regiment of the British Army, to the attention of the public in the most dramatic way possible – in the full glare of the international media.

feelings of doubt and fear had now disappeared. I was blasted. The adrenalin was bursting through my bloodstream. Fearsome! I got a fearsome rush, the best one of my life. I had the heavy body armour on, with high-velocity plates front and back. During training it weighs a ton. Now it felt like a T-shirt. Search and destroy!

His team had made its way into the library. It was dim and condensation on his respirator diminished visibility even further. It was just as well, he thought, that an explosive charge had not been used, for the books, of which there were hundreds, would have caught fire.

With the stairs cleared the men worked their way down into the cellar. Pulling the pin from a stun grenade, Winner tossed it down the stairs, then descended amidst the blinding flashes, all the while keeping an intensely sharp eye out for movement. Once in the corridor at the bottom the team moved methodically from room to room. With a sledgehammer or Remington shotgun, it was necessary to blow in the locks before kicking in the door. Winner loosed off a burst of 20 rounds at a crouched figure in the corner of a darkened room, only to discover afterwards that it was a dustbin.

Evacuating the hostages

The rooms having been cleared, the SAS men began assembling in a line on the main staircase where they roughly manhandled the hostages downstairs and out of the back of the embassy as quickly as possible. Some of the women were screaming and hysterical; most of the hostages were shocked, confused or frightened, tears running from their eyes as a result of the CS gas hanging in the air. As the hostages reached the bottom of the stairs, the soldiers began directing them out of the rear of the building.

In the course of this procession, however, one figure, having hidden amongst the hostages in the telex room, was identified as a terrorist, masquerading as a hostage. He ran the gauntlet of soldiers down the stairs, receiving kicks and blows as he went, crouching as best he could. Winner recorded what happened next:

He drew level with me. Then I saw it – a Russian fragmentation grenade. I could see the detonator cap protruding from his hand. I moved my hands to the MP 5 and slipped the safety-catch to 'automatic'. Through the smoke and gloom I could see call signs at the bottom of the stairs in the hallway. Sh**! I can't fire. They are in my line of sight, the bullets will go straight through the terrorist and into my mates. I've got to immobilize the bastard. Instinctively, I raised the MP5 above my head and in one swift,

Overleaf

SAS troopers bundling hostages down the stairs of the embassy to the ground floor, in the course of which a terrorist, masquerading as a hostage and clutching a grenade, is struck by quick-thinking Staff Sergeant Pete Winner, who used the stock of his MP5 instead of risking innocent lives by firing. It was in such circumstances, in the close proximity of a terrorist, where training in Close Quarter Battle (CQB) reaped its rewards. CQB had been developed since the 1960s, involving armed and unarmed fighting. In the case of the former, techniques in the use of both primary weapons (sub-machine guns) and secondary firearms (pistols) were honed to a fine edge, including movement, firing off the ground, and weapons stoppages (a jam which prevents discharge). In unarmed combat, CQB techniques included identification of points of attack on the body, and the means of protecting oneself from an assailant.

Fire rages on the first floor of the embassy only minutes after the teams burst in. Two Metropolitan Police officers, deployed to cover the assault team, squat on the balcony of the adjoining building. Shots echoed through the embassy even after the hostages had been found, as SAS teams used shotguns to blast away door locks in search of any remaining terrorists. (Getty)

sharp movement brought the stock of the weapon down on the back of his neck. I hit him as hard as I could. His head snapped backwards and for one fleeting second I caught sight of his tortured, hate-filled face. He collapsed forward and rolled down the remaining few stairs, hitting the carpet in the hallway, a sagging, crumpled heap. The sound of two magazines being emptied into him was deafening. As he twitched and vomited his life away, his hand opened and the grenade rolled out. In that split second my mind was so crystal clear with adrenalin it zoomed straight in on the grenade pin and lever. I stared at the mechanism for what seemed like an eternity, and what I saw flooded the very core of me with relief and elation. The pin was still located in the lever. It was all over, everything was going to be OK.

Almost immediately came the order by radio for the SAS teams to evacuate the building through the library entrance at the rear. The floors above were on fire and the rooms were all clear. It was time to leave. Emerging through the smoke, the men turned left towards no. 14, passing the sledgehammer used to batter in the door, and the unused explosive charge and other debris of the attack left on the ground. The hostages were led out to the gardens behind the building, laid out on the grass and bound with plastic straps, there to await identification. The women were aware of the presence of a terrorist, but refused to identify him. Sim Harris recognized him though, and he was led away, wounded. Inside the embassy, five of the terrorists lay dead: Oan in a room on the first floor, two in the telex room, one at the foot of the stairs near the front door on the ground floor and one in an office at the back of the building. One of the hostages had been killed by the terrorists during the assault, and two others had been injured. It had all taken just 17 minutes. In the Cabinet Office Briefing Room, where de la Billière had been monitoring radio traffic between the men as events unfolded, the place erupted in joy, as de la Billière recalled: 'Tension snapped. Papers flew in the air. Everyone leapt up, shouting and laughing. A roar of talk broke out. Bottles of whisky appeared from some secret cupboard, and we all had a much-needed drink.'

Once the siege had ended, control of the area was passed back from Army to civilian control, while firefighters began to tackle the blaze. The assault teams, meanwhile, quickly returned to no. 14, where they began to remove their assault kits and pack them into their holdalls. At the same time, their MP5s were sealed into plastic bags for later forensic examination. To this end, police investigators and forensic scientists would later enter the gutted building to begin reconstructing exactly what had happened; specifically, to examine the dead and conduct ballistics analysis of the ammunition and weapons used in the raid. The SAS men had been warned by an Army legal team before the assault that they had to use 'minimum force'; otherwise, they risked legal action against them for being overzealous. Part of the police investigation that was to follow was therefore intended to determine whether or not excessive force had in fact been employed.

Back at no. 14, mental and physical exhaustion now kicked in. Pete Winner recalled feeling '... the tiredness spreading through my limbs. It wasn't just energy expended on the assault, it was the accumulation of six days of tension and high drama, of snatched sleep in a noisy room, of anxiety and worry over the outcome of the operation.' PC Lock's wife then arrived to thank the men repeatedly for having saved her husband's life. At about the same time, the Home Secretary entered the room to offer his congratulations, his eyes filled with tears of joy and relief. 'This operation will show that we in Britain will not tolerate terrorists. The world must learn this.' The men appreciated his words: it was a fitting end to a successful operation. The men of both teams, together with intelligence officers and others, stood drinking lager from cans, the atmosphere buzzing with elation.

Then an unexpected visitor arrived. A dapper man in a pinstriped suit announced the Prime Minister, on whose entry the room fell silent and all attention turned in her direction. 'Gentlemen,' she said, 'there is nothing sweeter than success, and you boys have got it.' On this, cheers broke out and new cans of lager were opened. The Prime Minister gave a heartfelt speech, expressing pride at the superb handling of the assault, the product of brilliant teamwork and bravery. She and her husband then circulated among the men, thanking them all personally. At 2200hrs a television was wheeled in for all to see the drama played out on the news. When the Prime Minister appeared to block the view of those in the back, she was unceremoniously told to sit down. She did so, cross-legged on the floor. The programme was watched, the Prime Minister recalled, 'with a running commentary, punctuated by relieved laughter, from those involved in the assault. One of them turned to me and said, "We never thought you'd let us do it."'

Part of the post-operational procedure: with the siege over and the building cleared, the hostages are being processed on the lawn at the back of the embassy. All hostages are handcuffed until identified.

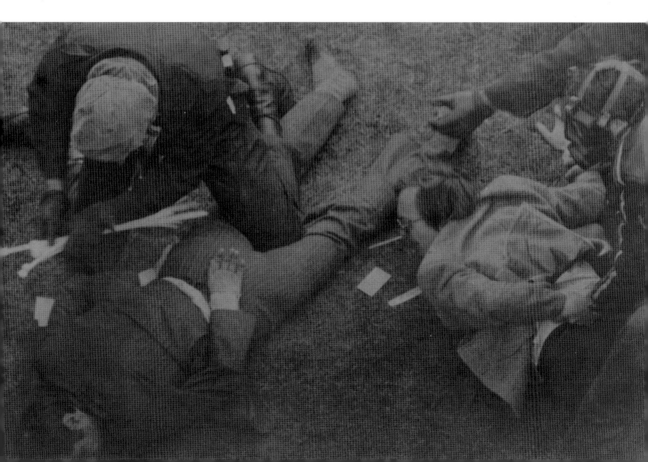

ANALYSIS

Operation *Nimrod* was an almost unqualified success: of a total of 26 hostages, two had been killed (in both cases by the terrorists), five had been released before the assault and 19 had been rescued. The police had done a superb job obtaining the release of a handful of hostages while keeping the remaining ones alive through prolonged negotiation. COBR, too, functioned extremely effectively, as Whitelaw acknowledged in his memoirs: 'My first impression was that I had to hand a first-class and highly efficient organization which appeared to have assembled at the drop of a hat. Once again I was struck by the immense administrative efficiency of our senior servants.' The gas board, for instance, immediately complied with the request for the creation of ambient noise in Princes Gate. So, too, did the Airports Authority, when Rose requested low-flying aircraft over the scene to conceal the work of technicians and engineers seeking to embed listening devices in the walls of the embassy.

1   Perched on the roof, assault teams abseil down the rear of the building, in the course of which a trooper inadvertently breaks a window with his boot, arousing the terrorists' suspicions that something is amiss.

2   As a diversionary tactic, SAS explosives experts lower a powerful charge through the central glass dome, detonating it moments before simultaneous assaults are launched against the front and rear of the embassy.

3   A team leader's abseil rope becomes snarled, abruptly halting his descent, suspending him helplessly above the second-floor rear balcony, and thus obliging the other members of his team to forego the use of frame charges and smash their way through the windows with hooligan bars. Stun grenades set fire to the curtains and carpet, causing flames to emerge from the windows and burn the entangled trooper.

4   An assault team crosses into the garden, smashes its way through the french doors leading into the library and proceeds to clear the ground floor and cellar, which are discovered unoccupied.

5   Crossing from an adjacent building, an assault team detonates frame charges against the armoured windows on the front balcony, throws in stun grenades and enters the building amidst billowing smoke.

6   While PC Lock and the terrorist leader, Oan, are locked in mortal combat in a room on the first floor, an SAS trooper from the front assault team bursts in, warns the constable off and shoots Oan with a burst from his MP5.

7   One of the rear assault teams, shooting dead one terrorist as he flees towards the front of the embassy, reaches the telex room, where three terrorists have managed to kill one hostage and injure two others only moments before. The SAS men dispatch two terrorists with automatic fire but fail to recognise the presence of the third, who masquerades as a hostage and retains possession of a hand grenade.

8   The female hostages, discovered unguarded in a room on the second floor, are hurriedly joined with their now liberated male counterparts and manhandled downstairs for evacuation out of the rear of the embassy.

9   Clutching a hand grenade and still concealed amongst the hostages as they are hustled downstairs, the undetected terrorist from the telex room is recognized by Staff Sergeant Pete Winner who, unable to open fire for fear of inflicting casualties on the hostages or his colleagues, strikes the terrorist on the back of the head with the butt of his weapon, causing his victim to tumble to the base of the stairway where other SAS men riddle him with machine-gun fire.

10 (Not visible) Frightened and confused, the rescued hostages emerge into the garden at the rear of the embassy, where their SAS escort place them face down on the ground, secure their wrists, and identify them, thus discovering and arresting the only surviving terrorist of the original six.

Fire damage caused by the detonation of the frame charge placed against the front balcony window. The siege was probably nearing its conclusion when this photograph was taken.

As for Whitelaw himself, he was later praised by de la Billière:

[I had regarded] Willie Whitelaw as no more than a jovial, avuncular figure. Now I had reason to change my opinion. From the start he handled those difficult meetings with calm, incisive authority, which reminded everyone present that during the Second World War he had served with distinction as an officer in the Scots Guards. Never autocratic, he let people have their say, yet always brought a discussion to an end with a firm decision, leaving nothing in the air.

Success could be measured in other terms, as well. British authorities had conceded very little: while they did broadcast the terrorists' message, they never supplied the requested Arab mediators, and thus avoided handing the initiative over to others who might have made concessions unauthorized by Downing Street. In the end, the siege was not a drawn-out affair and safe conduct for the gunmen was never supplied. Nor did the Government rush to employ force. The Cabinet Office was initially concerned with longer-term contingency plans and with the possible international repercussions. But it is essential to understand that the primary objective of such an operation is to secure the unconditional safe release of the hostages through peaceful persuasion. This was the rationale behind the long and sometimes frustrating exchanges between the police negotiators and the terrorists. But it was undoubtedly worth pursuing as the procedure had been successfully used on previous occasions and was well practised within the police.

As he had promised, Whitelaw did not interfere in the execution of the actual assault, quite properly devolving authority to those best equipped to direct and carry it out. Similarly, the Prime Minister, in choosing not to appear at COBR meetings and having delegated authority to the Home Secretary, did not interfere in the business of the committee he chaired. As de la Billière put it, 'a supreme commander – civilian or military – must delegate authority if he is to get the best out of his people.'

Nor did the Army exceed its legal brief by operating outside its authority, as de la Billière explained: 'The chain of command was complex but clearly defined. As always in the United Kingdom, police primacy remained absolute: the Army could act only if the Home Secretary authorized it to do so.' And that is precisely what happened. In short, much of the success of the operation rested on the fact that civil–military relations remained on a proper footing throughout, with all levels respecting the chain of command and accepting that, having confidently devolved authority downwards, all those involved were to be allowed to carry out their tasks without interference.

There were, of course, those who criticized the government for not using force earlier, but Whitelaw outlined why patience and forbearance were the watchwords of the day:

> The critics thought that the SAS should have been sent in much earlier. I believe that this criticism ignores the main objective in handling such incidents, which must always be the release of the hostages unharmed but without conceding the terrorists' demands. Therefore all efforts at peaceful persuasion must be exhausted. That is the task of the police negotiators. If they fail, and before force is used, all the possible consequences of action by the SAS or other troops must be accepted before the order for their deployment is given.

> Those who give the orders have to recognize that troops have an immensely difficult role when used in the twilight area between peace and war, euphemistically described as action in support of the civil power... All too often the immediate benefit of the troops' action is quickly forgotten. Then, after considerable delay, come the legal proceedings accompanied by accusations of excessive force and unnecessary loss of life. These in turn increasingly expose the Government, which has been protecting its citizens, and its troops to substantial criticism at the bar of the world media. As a result wicked and violent organizations achieve propaganda success and increased financial support. All these repercussions may seem tiresome... But free nations do not have that option since they proclaim, rightly, that they are upholding freedom under the law. They cannot pick and choose when to do so themselves.

William (Willie) Whitelaw, the Home Secretary, according to whom, 'The SAS operation had been a complete and dramatic success. This said much for their professional skill and courage.' (Getty)

When, however, the options had been truly exhausted and the negotiating phase had come to an end, the SAS, armed with the requisite skills, training, courage and weaponry had done the rest. More significantly the SAS dealt with a number of unexpected problems throughout the course of the raid.

1. During the ascent at the rear of the building, one abseiler broke a window with his boot, alerting the terrorists of the attack and obliging the teams at the rear of the building to open the assault before the team on the first-floor front balcony was ready to detonate its explosive charge. However, the mistiming of the assault did not in fact jeopardize the operation; surprise was not unduly compromised and both teams made successful entries into the embassy.
2. Sergeant Tommy Palmer became caught in his rope, receiving serious burns from a fire that broke out as Red Team made a forcible entry. This incident rendered impossible the ability of the team on the ground to blow in the rear ground-floor windows as intended, being unable to use explosives for fear of injuring their stricken comrade. The soldier concerned suffered first-degree burns to his feet and legs, which were left dangling in front of the flames emerging from the second-floor window. However, he was rapidly cut down by other members of his team who successfully entered the embassy and reached the telex room. It is worth noting that Palmer continued the assault despite the fact that he had to remove his protective hood once it caught fire and he had no protection from smoke and CS gas. After the raid he was treated for his burns injuries at St Stephen's Hospital in Fulham and made a full recovery.

3. Palmer's MP5 jammed in the act of firing at a terrorist. However, he was able to successfully chase down the terrorist and use his pistol.

4. As a result of the carpets having been doused with an inflammable substance by the terrorists, fire broke out when the assault teams detonated explosive charges against the front first-floor windows. Stun grenades thrown into both the front and rear windows of the embassy may also have contributed to the outbreak of fire. The fires rapidly communicated with the drapes, spreading the flames and endangering the lives of those within. Although the SAS were unaware of the presence of what appeared to be kerosene, there was perhaps no alternative to the use of explosives to facilitate entry into a structure fortified by armoured glass. In any event, success was achieved with such rapidity that the occupants of the building suffered no injuries as a result and the flames were brought under control by the fire brigade in the aftermath of the assault.

Tom the Fijian (top right), his rope jammed in the harness clog, suspends helplessly just moments before flames emerge from the window to engulf his legs. On the extreme left Tommy Palmer has just arrived on the second-floor balcony, still attached to his abseil rope. Note the torch mounted on the MP5 held by the trooper beside him.

The success of the operation may also be attributed to a major error on the part of the terrorists. They had failed to deploy any effective booby traps, tripwires or other countermeasures to prevent forcible entry. Nor had they, as they claimed, rigged the building with high explosives. Had they done so, large-scale injury and death may have resulted. The inexperience of the terrorists therefore played a part in their downfall, as did their failure to kill the hostages once the assault had started. Indeed,

as the assault played out on live television on a bank holiday and in front of a huge audience, the stunning success of the SAS captured the imagination of the world. It is easy to forget that the result could have just as easily been a massive propaganda victory for the hostage-takers if heavy casualties had resulted.

Effects on the SAS

Despite the overwhelming success achieved by the SAS, the raid brought unwanted public attention to a hitherto virtually unknown regiment of the British Army. As one soldier who took part, known only as 'J', recalled,

> Princes Gate was a turning point. It demonstrated to the powers that be what the Regiment could do and just what an asset the country had, but it also brought a problem we wished to avoid: the media spotlight. In addition, for the first few years after the siege selection courses were packed with what seemed like every man in the British Army wanting to join the SAS. We just couldn't cope with the numbers who were applying, and so we had to introduce extra physicals on the first day just to get rid of the wasters. The same problem affected R Squadron, the reserve, and the sergeant in charge was overwhelmed with recruits. (Crawford, *The SAS at Close Quarters*, p. 79)

Specifically, while membership of 22 SAS is possible only by the transfer of serving personnel from existing Army units, the Territorial regiment, 21 SAS, was swamped by hundreds of aspirants outside the gates of their Headquarters in the Kings Road, 'all', according to de la Billière, 'apparently convinced that a balaclava helmet and a Heckler & Koch sub-machine gun would be handed to them over the counter, so that they could go off and conduct embassy-style sieges of their own.' The numbers rapidly declined when, in the first phase of training, the CO, Keith Farnes, put them on a running track and watched as all but a handful collapsed in exhaustion. In short, success brought instant publicity, which was never courted.

For the SAS the rescue of the embassy hostages justified the years of training and vindicated those who had long defended the need for the regiment's continued existence. Wild notions by conspiracy theorists that the regiment, in its counter-revolutionary role, might somehow seek to overthrow the civilian government, were shown to be laughable. Success, moreover, did much to counter the negative image that had been actively propagated by the IRA for several years prior to the raid.

Its role, as originally outlined by Stirling, could carry on as before because the regiment would remain intact; specifically, the result of the siege fully justified the establishment of the Special Projects Team, which carried out the assault with a surprisingly small number of men, for only about 30 to 35 actually took a direct part. In addition, there was a five-man command group consisting of the OC of B Squadron, the squadron Sergeant-Major, the intelligence officer, and two signallers. There was also a reserve team of eight troopers who were not committed to the assault. A politically fragile situation with potentially disastrous consequences was defused in a matter of minutes, and thus the seven years of careful thought, analysis, rehearsal and training were shown to have been worthwhile.

There were no adverse legal consequences for the SAS as a result of the assault; as discussed, immediately after the raid the soldiers sealed their weapons in bags, labelled them and turned them over to the police, who held them until a coroner's inquiry could be held. The following morning, detectives flew to Hereford, where they spent thirty-six hours interviewing and taking statements from members of the team to create an exhaustive record of where and when every shot had been fired. At the inquest held some months later four soldiers, identified only by letters and avoiding photographers, gave evidence. At the trial of the surviving terrorist, the same questions were asked to determine if excessive force had been used. De la Billière observed that:

On the day there was no time for the luxury of reflection: Mike Rose's brief was to rescue the hostages alive, and he and his team did it brilliantly. Nevertheless, at the inquest we were concerned that if the evidence failed to justify what we had done, our people could hit trouble.

In the event, this did not happen, but the possibility that it could emphasized an important point: just because a Minister authorizes a soldier to do something, that man may not break the law. A Minister had no right to set aside the law; nor does the Brigadier or the Commanding Officer of the SAS. In fighting terrorism, we repeatedly put our soldiers into very difficult positions: on the one hand they are being told to combat terrorism in the streets, but on the other they are still subject to the law of the land, and may not shoot anyone except under precisely defined circumstances. If we had gone into the Iranian Embassy earlier before the terrorists killed anyone, and provoked the death of hostages by starting a battle, we should have been in grave trouble.

Opposite

The potentially disastrous moment when the operation went badly – though not irretrievably – wrong. The abseiler at top right is Tom the Fijian, his full descent prevented by his rope having jammed in the harness clog. Suspended in this position, his legs dangle amidst the flames while the trooper below him tries to cut him down. The abseiler on the extreme left is Tommy Palmer, bareheaded after he was obliged to cast off his gas hood and respirator after they caught fire. He has just spotted a terrorist in the room setting the carpet alight. Seconds after this photo was taken Palmer jumped into the room, took a bead on the terrorist and squeezed the trigger, only to hear the 'dead man's click': a first round stoppage. He therefore drew his pistol, chased the man down the corridor, and shot him in the head, just as the terrorist was about to pull the pin on a grenade and lob it into the Telex Room amongst the male hostages. For this act Palmer was awarded the Queen's Gallantry Medal.

Observations on the terrorists

What can be said of the mindset and expectations of the terrorists? It appears that the hostage-takers had been poorly briefed by their handlers about the irresolution they were likely to encounter on the part of the British government. The gunmen seem to have nurtured completely unrealistic expectations of success. Judging by the extent of their shopping in the weeks prior to the attack on the embassy, there is no doubt that they expected to return safely to Iraq. They were not highly trained; only their leader, Oan, could speak English tolerably well, and he would make use of the Pakistani journalist to translate much of his statements into English. The extent to which the terrorists' minders in Iraq properly prepared them for the operation is not known, but it seemed an amateurish affair. All evidence suggests the terrorists thought the operation would be over in 48 hours, with the police doing nothing, the government inept and the risk to the gunmen minimal. Their cause would be widely publicized, they would receive at least a modicum of diplomatic recognition – albeit perhaps fleeting – from the Arab ambassadors who were to mediate with them, and make an unhindered journey back to Iraq where, presumably, they expected rewards and recognition for their achievement.

They did not appear to have had any military training, for, according to the hostages, they handled their grenades with dangerous incompetence, and they appeared not to have been briefed about the consequences of taking the life of a hostage – an act which invariably signals the end of any possibility of further useful negotiation with the authorities. In short, the murder of a hostage reduced the options to just two: prison or death in a shoot-out.

Long-term impact

It is important to recognize that in the background of the siege lay political problems separate from the military ones facing the SAS as it planned an assault. The lives of the American hostages in Iran were possibly at stake just as were those of the Iranian hostages in London. Quite apart from the original motives behind the seizure of the American Embassy in Tehran, Iranian officials were persuaded that the siege in London was nothing more than an American-backed plot to pressure Iran into releasing its American prisoners, now that American military means had failed to rescue them. In such a situation, it was plausible that the British Embassy in Tehran, or British nationals in Iran, might be taken prisoner, or that the American diplomats would be harmed or put on trial. All this must be seen in the context of the failed attempt by US Special Forces to rescue the American hostages only weeks before the embassy siege in London when, on the night of 24–25 April, Delta Force lost eight killed and several helicopters destroyed in the attempt.

Iranian propaganda was already heightening tension, with radio broadcasts in Tehran falsely claiming that the hostages in London had smuggled out a note declaring their willingness to die as martyrs for the Islamic Revolution. If that martyrdom came as a result of a bungled British police or military operation, the government in Tehran might take action against Westerners accordingly. Thus, much more hung on the outcome of the siege apart from the lives of the hostages themselves: the competence of the British government and, specifically, Margaret Thatcher's credibility, the lives of the American hostages in Iran and the possible escalation of tensions – even open hostilities – between the USA and Iran, already operating at a high pitch.

The success of the operation was a stark warning to other potential hostage-takers that London was not a safe area for such activity. As Whitelaw later wrote in his memoirs, 'We in Britain had shown the world that we were prepared to take a stand against terrorists, and indeed to defeat them. There can be no greater deterrent to future action than that.' The successful outcome of the crisis also increased overseas demand by police and counter-terrorist units for information about SAS training and techniques. The British government duly took advantage of this, sending SAS teams abroad to train their counterparts in friendly countries, a task which strengthened political ties and benefited the Treasury.

Above all other consequences of the raid must stand its impact on the minds of the millions of people watching the drama unfold on live television. This cannot be underestimated, for it created a degree of pride perhaps unseen since VE Day. That feeling of course defied measurement, but it was pervasive, forming the subject of many a conversation and filling columns of newspaper editorials. In short, success for the SAS had translated itself into success for the nation as a whole. As the Prime Minister related in her memoirs: 'Wherever I went over the next few days, I sensed a great wave of pride at the outcome; telegrams of congratulation poured in from abroad: we had sent a signal to terrorists everywhere that they could expect no deals and would extort no favours from Britain.'

The nation as a whole experienced a rush of patriotism, precisely at a time when it needed it most: the USA had just failed to rescue its diplomats held illegally in Iran; the Soviets had invaded Afghanistan only months before, leaving the West powerless to respond; the IRA's campaign of terrorism in Northern Ireland showed no signs of abatement; at home, inflation was rising and industrial action was commonplace. All these events left the impression, when coupled with the seizure of the Iranian Embassy in London, that the West was impotent and on the decline. The successful outcome of the assault burst this bubble in a matter of minutes and restored the pride of millions in their nation.

GLOSSARY

Alpha Control	The main forward control point established by the police at 24 Princes Gate
Ammunition	The SAS required ammunition that could neutralize opponents with a minimum of risk to hostages and allies. The standard 9mm round does not always stop on impact and can pass through the target and strike a bystander. To reduce this risk, SAS teams carried rounds specifically designed to break up inside the target's body or to flatten on impact. Ammunition for shotguns was the Hatton round, a 12-bore cartridge with a bullet head made of a soft material whose kinetic energy disperses on impact, designed to rip off a door hinge with reduced risk to a room's occupants
Assault suit	A one-piece garment worn over body armour, made of flame-resistant, anti-static, liquid-repellent black fabric. The suit was fastened by a full-length, two-way zip, protected by a storm flap, with knitted cuffing at the collar, wrists and ankles. The areas around the forearms, knees and shins were reinforced with quilted fabric surrounding flame-resistant felt, providing extra protection against heat. The suit was also fitted with a drag-handle, enabling the soldier, if unconscious or unable to move, to be dragged to safety
Body armour	Designed for assault roles, it accommodated differing grades of ballistic protection, and could include a groin protector. Pockets in front and rear allowed for the insertion of ceramic plates as protection against high velocity small-arms ordnance
Bradbury Lines	Original name of the SAS barracks at Hereford, established in 1960 as the headquarters of 22 SAS; shortly after the Iranian Embassy siege the new barracks were built and the entire site renamed Stirling Lines, in honour of the regiment's founder, David Stirling
Browning 9mm	Of 1920s British design now manufactured in Belgium, it holds an unusually large, 13-round magazine. An exceptionally reliable reserve weapon
Call sign	The signal assigned to a particular soldier or unit that serves to identify it
COBR	Cabinet Office Briefing Room; situation room in a basement in Whitehall in which senior government officials, led by the Home Secretary, manage an internal crisis, such as a major terrorist incident. Director SAS is normally in attendance to brief the committee on the regiment's state of readiness and the manner in which it can be deployed
CRW	Counter-revolutionary Warfare; the full name of the SAS training wing, which, working around the world, specializes in training counter-terrorist teams, infiltrating enemy organizations, gathering intelligence, carrying out ambushes, performing demolition work, and providing bodyguards for VIPs abroad

CQB	Close Quarter Battle; technique of fighting in a confined space, such as a room or vehicle
CQB House	Close Quarter Battle House; better known as 'the Killing House', located at SAS HQ in Hereford, where the SAS conducts part of its anti-terrorist training
CS gas	Canister smoke gas, deployed to confuse the enemy by obscuring his view
D11	Metropolitan Police elite firearms team
'double tap'	To fire two rounds from a handgun in rapid succession; in 1980, two shots to the head were believed sufficient to kill a terrorist or hostage-taker, but sustained fire is now preferred in cases where a remote detonation device is suspected
figure-eleven target	Practice target on firing range
'flash bang'	Stun grenade. On detonation, it emits a deafening noise (160 Db), an extremely bright light (300,000cd), and a cloud of smoke, stunning and disorienting anyone close by for approximately 3 to 5 seconds, with no risk of fragmentation, as little metal is used in its largely cardboard casing
frame charge	A wooden frame to which a metal-cased explosive is attached for the purpose of blowing a hole through a wall or destroying armoured glass; the SAS used a custom-made version to fit the dimensions of a window on the first-floor front of the embassy
gloves	Specially-designed assault gloves made of a black flame-resistant and waterproof fabric, to protect the wearer's hands, but also providing free finger movement. Each glove had a soft leather trigger finger and, to protect against friction burns during abseiling, soft reversed-calf leather on the palm
green slime	Nickname for Intelligence Corps (named for their distinctive green berets)
Heckler & Koch MP5	West German-made 9mm sub-machine gun, known to the SAS as the 'Hockler' or 'HK'. Light and short, it can be set to automatic fire or single shot. Firing with a closed and locked bolt mechanism, with a delayed blowback action, it has better safety and accuracy than most other sub-machine guns
IA	Immediate Action; a plan of assault to be implemented without delay (for example, in response to the shooting of hostages) in circumstances where the SAS, having just been deployed, is unable to assess the situation with the benefit of time and intelligence-gathering
ISFE	Instantaneous safety-fuse electric
'Killing House'	Informal name for the Close Quarter Battle (CQB) House where the SAS practises some of its anti-terrorist operations
Kremlin	Nickname for the operations centre at SAS regimental headquarters, Hereford
OC	Officer Commanding
Operation *Nimrod*	Codename for the SAS operations against the Iranian Embassy
Pagoda	Codename for the SAS counter-terrorist team
PE	Plastic explosives; prepared charge used to gain entry into a building, such as through bullet-proof or armoured glass, or

aircraft or other vehicle; PE can be fashioned into a frame for use against a window

Regent's Park Barracks
An Army facility off Albany Street, in London, which served as the SAS's main base for the whole of the siege

Remington 870 shotgun
12-gauge (2.75 inch/70mm) shotgun used to blast away the lock or hinges from a door. It weighed 3.6kg and carried 7 rounds

Respirator
Specifically designed for use in counter-terrorist operations, the S6 respirator, or 'gas mask', was fitted with a CS filter canister to protect the wearer from CS, CR and other irritant gases. The rubber face-piece was fitted with removable coated polycarbonate tinted glass lenses which provided protection from the flash of 'flash-bangs', as well as from fragments. The mask also contained a high-quality speech transmitter. A second canister mount allowed another form of radio communications or could be used with a second filter canister, if needed, or with a small bottle of compressed air which could provide oxygen in instances where smoke or fumes would otherwise incapacitate the wearer

Sabre Squadron
Combat or fighting squadron of an SAS regiment; 22 SAS has four: A, B, D and G; a squadron contains approximately 60 men, divided into four troops, together with a small headquarters section. Each patrol within a troop consists of four men, the basic sub-unit of the SAS, with each man possessing a particular skill, such as in signals, demolition, facility in a foreign language, or medical expertise, in addition to the basic skills acquired by all troopers in the course of their training

SAS
Special Air Service; the regiment associated with the Embassy siege is 22 SAS, as opposed to 21 and 23, which are Territorial Army units; the regiment consists of four squadrons, A, B, D and G, with, in 1980, a reserve, 'R' squadron (now 'L' Detachment), which is a Territorial Army reserve unit. The regiment includes a number of other squadrons for training, signals, intelligence, and various sub-sections tasked with regimental administration

SP Team
Special Projects Team; the full, official name of the SAS anti-hijack/counter-terrorism team

Stirling Lines
The present-day name of the headquarters of 22 SAS, near Hereford; known, until shortly after the embassy siege, as Bradbury Lines

Stronghold
Name given by the police to the occupied embassy

thunderflash
grenade-simulator

wash-up
De-briefing of an SAS team in the wake of a siege-breaking exercise

FURTHER READING

Bishop, Patrick, *From SAS to Sarajevo: The Biography of Lt. Gen. Sir Michael Rose* (Bantam Press, London, 1995)

Brock, George, *Siege: Six Days at the Iranian Embassy* (Macmillan, London, 1980)

Brown, Ashley (ed.), *Elite Forces: The SAS* (Orbis, London, 1986)

Chant, Christopher, *SAS in Action* (Parragon Plus, London, 1997)

Connor, Ken, *Ghost Force: The Secret History of the SAS* (Cassell, London, 2006)

Crawford, Steve, *The SAS at Close Quarters* (Sidgwick & Jackson, London, 1993)

Crawford, Steve, *The SAS Encyclopedia* (Simon & Schuster, London, 1996)

Darman, Peter, *A–Z of the SAS* (Sidgwick & Jackson, London, 1993)

Darman, Peter, *Weapons and Equipment of the SAS* (Sidgwick & Jackson, London, 1994)

Davies, Barry, *The Complete Encyclopedia of the SAS* (Virgin Books, London, 2001)

Davies, Barry, *SAS Rescue* (Sidgwick & Jackson, London, 1997)

Davies, Barry, *SAS: Shadow Warriors of the 21st century. The Special Air Service Anti-terrorist Team* (Spellmount, Staplehurst, Kent, 2002)

de la Billière, Peter, *Looking for Trouble: SAS to Gulf Command* (HarperCollins, London, 1995)

Fowler, William, *SAS and Special Forces* (Collins, London, 1996)

Garnett, Mark and Aitken, Ian, *Splendid! Splendid!: The Life and Times of Willie Whitelaw* (Jonathan Cape, London, 2002)

Geraghty, Tony, *This is the SAS: A Pictorial History of the SAS* (Fontana, London, 1983)

Geraghty, Tony, *Who Dares Wins: The Special Air Service, 1950 to the Gulf War* (Abacus, London, 2002)

Hunter, Robin, *True Stories of the SAS* (Virgin Books, London, 1995)

Kemp, Anthony, *The SAS: Savage Wars of Peace, 1947 to the Present* (Penguin, London, 2001)

Ladd, James, *SAS Operations: More than Daring* (Robert Hale, London, 1989)

Macdonald, Peter, *The SAS in Action* (Sidgwick & Jackson, London, 1990)

McAleese, Peter and Avery, John, *McAleese's Fighting Manual* (Orion, London, 1998)

Newsinger, John, *Dangerous Men: The SAS and Popular Culture* (Pluto Press, London, 1997)

Philip, Craig and Taylor, Alex, *Inside the SAS* (Bloomsbury, London, 1994)

Ratcliffe, Peter, *Eye of the Storm: Twenty-five Years in Action with the SAS* (Michael O'Mara, London, 2003)

Scholey, Pete, *SAS Heroes: Remarkable Soldiers, Extraordinary Men* (Osprey Publishing, Oxford, 2008)

Stewart, Graeme, *Silent Heroes: The Story of the SAS* (Michael O'Mara, London, 1997)

Strawson, John, *A History of the SAS Regiment* (Secker & Warburg, London, 1984)

Sunday Times 'Insight' Team, *Siege! Princes Gate, London – The Great Embassy Rescue* (HMSO, London, 1984)

Thatcher, Margaret, *The Downing Street Years* (HarperCollins, London, 1995)

Warner, Philip, *The Special Air Service* (Time-Warner Books, New York, 1991)

Weale, Adrian, *The Real SAS* (Pan, London, 1999)

Whitelaw, William, *The Whitelaw Memoirs* (Aurum Press, London, 1989)

INDEX

References to illustrations are shown in **bold**.